*Hajin Lee*

# *Outside the Board*

HAJIN LEE

# OUTSIDE THE BOARD

DIARY OF A PROFESSIONAL GO PLAYER

OLD HICKORY PRESS

2016

*Outside the Board.*
*by Hajin Lee*

Designed & typeset by Andrew Jackson.
Cover design by Dan Maas.

Thanks to Andy Okun & Judy Debel
for additional proofreading.

First printing, 2016.

Old Hickory Press, LLC
700 NE 45th St,
Seattle, WA. 98105
www.oldhickorypress.org

Trade Hardcover ISBN
978-1-945025-01-3

# Contents

## I   Professional Life in Seoul

## II   Different Worlds

## III  University

# IV    Management in Go

# Appendix

# *Introduction*

When I studied Go for seven to ten hours a day, I had one clear life goal: To become a professional Go player. The competition to become a pro is tough - less than one tenth of all prodigies pass the threshold. Most prodigies devote their lives to improving their Go skills, and having any other dream is considered a distraction.

Even so, I had a secret dream that I didn't tell anyone. I wanted to become a writer. Reading books was my favorite hobby, and once in a while I wrote short stories or essays for fun. Though none of my writings from that time were good enough to be published, I always thought I would publish at least one book in my life.

In 2008, I started a blog to practice writing in English and to share my life stories with the western Go community. I named my blog *Star Baduk*, because my name in Korean has the literal meaning "summer star". In it, I wrote more than 100 entries over about five years. These years were a transitional period for my career, from an active professional player to a university student, then from student to an administrator of an international Go organization. Due to that, my entries covered a wide area of my life from my personal memories, professional tournaments, travels, school life, and so on. As my life reached a faster and busier pace, though, I gradually moved my writing to emails and social media, and eventually I shut down my blog completely.

One day I was organizing files in my computer and noticed my old blog entries. Rereading them, they were not sophisticated, like ones written by a professional writer, but I found them genuine. As I read about my childhood stories and life as a professional player again, I thought it might be illuminating for Go players, especially those who follow professional players' games, but don't get to see much of their lives outside the board.

This is how I came to see my old entries as book material. Still, the book wouldn't have been possible without support from several people. My special thanks to Andrew Jackson, Fabien Lheureux, Andrew Okun, and Dan Maas. They were not only there as my best friends, but also edited my entries, gave me feedback, and helped me through the technical aspects of publishing. I would also like to thank my family for always being by my side.

I hope you enjoy the book and find inspiration to play more Go and appreciate more professional games!

# *Timeline*

## Part I
# Professional Life in Seoul

## Sweet Home

NOVEMBER 22ND 2008 — This is going to be my first entry, so let me introduce myself. My name is Hajin, and I am a professional baduk player. "Baduk" is the Korean name for Go, and I will be using Go and baduk interchangeably. I am 20 years old and living in Seoul, the capital city of Korea.

Living in Seoul can be exciting as long as you are young and not easily exhausted by the fast pace of everything. I like Seoul, especially its dynamic atmosphere and modern architecture. Just one thing is missing in Seoul, though, and that's my family.

My family lives in Daejeon, about 200 kilometers away from Seoul. Daejeon is located near the center of South Korea, and known for many universities and research institutions. I asked my parents a few times if they could move to Seoul in order to live with me, but they would always say they couldn't leave their jobs. Then, they would ask me back, "What if YOU came home?"

I would say no. What about my matches? My friends? My job? Lately, though, I had second thoughts about my answer. If we both insisted, would we ever get to live together? At this point I should tell you that I left my family when I was 9 years old. When I first moved to my baduk teacher's house, both my parents and I thought this separation would end when I become a professional player. But it turns out a professional player needs to live in Seoul, if she is serious about playing in tournaments. That is why I am still in Seoul, although I became pro about four years ago. On one hand, I am still young, and it seems I have plenty of time to share with my family. On the other hand, things are not likely to change, and time flies. Plus, it will become even more difficult to live with my family once I get married.

So, I have decided to move back to Daejeon! Although I will have no friends or nowhere to go, I will be living with my family again for the first time in 11 years. It actually feels like forever, as I was quite young when I left home. Family alone is not adequate in life. Yet, I am good at keeping myself busy. Surely I will find something in Daejeon, too. As for my matches, I will take KTX, the Korean express train, back to Seoul. On the KTX, it takes only one hour from Daejeon to Seoul. Most Korean professional tournaments start at 10 a.m., so my long commute should be manageable.

I came home yesterday to spend the weekend with my family and announce my decision. You can imagine how excited they were to learn the news. We had a small party with a bottle of wine and some fruit to celebrate our reunion. Along with that, we also celebrated the beginning of my blog.

I have been a big reader throughout my life, and I enjoy writing too. One day I told my dad that I would like to start a blog, and he offered to set up one for me with my own domain. We named my blog "Star Baduk" because in my name, "Jin" means star. Coincidentally, we also have nine "star points" on the Go board. On this blog, I plan to write about my daily life, thoughts, trips, or anything that comes to my life. My decision to move back to my parents' place will change my life, and writing a blog will be good for keeping things on track.

We haven't set a date for my move yet, but it should be sometime in Spring next year. For now, I will need to go back to Seoul to continue my life there.

# A Day With Kids

NOVEMBER 26TH 2008 — My life in Seoul has two major elements: professional matches and work. There are about 20 annual professional tournaments in Korea, most of them being single elimination. Thus, the number of matches you play annually depends on your average performance, and I play about 50 matches per year.

Other than playing matches, I've been working at the Y Baduk Academy (YBA) as a textbook writer for almost two years now. When I say I work at YBA, people often assume I teach baduk to the students. Yet, because I do my work on a computer at the office, I have minimum interaction with the students. The closest occasion would be going to lunch together in a big group once in a while. Even over lunch, though, the students like to talk to each other, not to me. I guess I am too old to be their friend. I don't mind it though. I feel uncomfortable with unpredictable things, and I find these young kids very unpredictable!

Today was a good example of that. It all began with the annual General Meeting of the Korean Professional Players' Union, which was held at the KBA (Korea Baduk Association) building today. This year's meeting drew a lot of attention because it included a few controversial agenda items such as a ranking system and a structure for prize money. All pros are invited, but I couldn't attend because I needed to stay at YBA. At YBA, there are one headmaster and three masters, and all four of them are senior professional players. Just as in any other meetings, the seniors shape important decisions at the professional players' union. So, I received the mission to take care of the students between 8 and 12 years old in the absence of the masters.

I naively assumed it would be nice to change for a day. Truth was, I had limited experience in teaching, and I didn't know what it would be like. I was a student all along, then I was a tournament player until I got this office job. In short, it was a disaster. I had to shout "be quiet!!", "don't do that!!", "focus" all the time. Kids would never stop talking and running around, testing my patience every minute. Then, even when I wanted to be strict, I didn't know how.

As I was struggling with these small students, I wondered if I was like them when I was their age. My baduk life began when I was 5 years old. My parents played baduk in our living room on holidays. My little sister was still a baby and I would watch my parents play and try to figure out what they were doing. One day my dad asked me if I wanted to learn how to play the game, and I gladly said yes.

I was an introvert. I enjoyed reading books and solving puzzles, feeling comfortable with a few close friends rather than in a big group. Baduk had every quality I liked, and I quickly got into the game. Another thing that kept me in baduk was going up in rank. One day my teacher told me I just got promoted to 13-kyu (I was 15-kyu). I was so excited about going up two levels at once that I danced all along on my way home, and woke up my mom from her nap so that I could tell her immediately.

Anyway, I don't remember talking and running around in my baduk classes! Why are these kids so different? Tomorrow, I will be grateful to return to my calm office work.

## Teaching Baduk in English

DECEMBER 2ND 2008 — There are two European students at the YBA, Alexa from Hungary and Javier from Finland. The two came to Korea to study baduk at the IBA (the International Baduk Academy - a baduk academy specifically for foreign players), but they decided to move to the YBA in order to experience more intense training. They told me later that the IBA was English friendly, but not as strict as other Korean baduk academies like the YBA.

When Alexa and Javier first came to YBA, the headmaster was hesitant about accepting them. He wasn't sure whether they could study all day (9 a.m. to 9 p.m.) with their limited Korean and thought their struggle might create a negative influence for other students. Yet the headmaster gave them a chance, and so far it seems he was right to do so. They are both studying hard and getting along well with our Korean students.

After some observation, the headmaster asked me if I would mind having a one-hour game review session with them in English, once a day. With this question, I knew the headmaster was convinced they would not be leaving anytime soon. I was tempted to come up with an excuse to say no, but I changed my mind and agreed to do it. Though working on a textbook at the office was my comfort zone, I was the only English speaker at YBA, and I wanted to help Alexa and Javier, who were going through hard training in a foreign country far from their own.

Many people assume that it is easy for me to teach baduk in English. After all, I am strong enough in baduk, and I can make myself understood in English. Yet, I found it challenging to teach baduk in English. More than anything, I got nervous when I did game reviews in English, forgetting words and expressions I should know.

Going through the first session with Alexa and Javier today, though, I realized something. It was my first time to actually teach baduk in English without having my English teacher observing me. With my teacher's presence, I couldn't get over the feeling that it was my English being evaluated, more than the quality of the review.

It was 2006 when I went to Europe for the first time. The world outside East Asia was amazing and I decided to study English so that I could visit Europe more and have meaningful interactions with European players. Once back in Korea, I started attending the Baduk English class. Professor Hahn and his wife, Professor Park, were running the class in Seoul for young baduk players who aspired to teaching baduk abroad. The class met twice a week, two hours per class. The first hour was for English grammar, and the second was for a game review. For the review session, all students were required to take a turn, one person per class. Every now and then my turn would come, and I would review one of my games in front of the class, using the English terms and expressions covered in the class. My classmates were mostly pros or strong amateur players. Thus, our focus was on the communication and use of English, rather than on the moves.

Actual teaching was different. Once the main object was to teach, English became secondary. My moves and their questions would already communicate without words, and they often understood everything when I showed them a move or a variation. When I needed explanations, I could use my English without too much difficulty.

So, it seems like I can teach in English now. I've been dreaming of this day since I came back from my first trip to Europe in 2006. On that trip I was frustrated so much because I didn't speak English. In Europe, I told myself more than a thousand times "I am going to study English when I go back to Korea." And, here I am, after two and a half years, teaching in English! It's still not perfect, but I am going to review their games tomorrow again and hopefully I will only get better.

## Victory

December 4$^{\text{TH}}$ 2008 — My job at YBA is conventional with eight working hours a day, five days a week. But, there is one special agreement. When I have a professional match, I get a free off-day. Well, it's not exactly "free", since my salary would have been higher if it weren't for this condition, but it's still a great deal for me. Otherwise I wouldn't have been able to have a job at all. Though it hasn't been easy, I am grateful that I could have my professional career and a stable job at the same time.

I am feeling exhausted, but also as proud as a general who just led a bloody war to a victory or a hobbit who just came back to his hobbit hole after going through a number of crazy adventures. Are you curious what happened? I played in the quarter final of the women's Kuksu title tournament today, and won! "Kuksu" is an ancient Korean word, meaning "The Hand of the Nation" and it refers to the strongest baduk player in the country. The Kuksu is one of the oldest and most prestigious titles that a professional player can achieve, and 14 years ago they started a separate Kuksu tournament for female pros only. The launch of this tournament didn't mean female players couldn't play in the general Kuksu tournament, though.

The game lasted over seven hours and it was really complicated the whole way through. You may be surprised at seven hours, but it's not uncommon for a pro match to last for even eight or nine hours. In traditional title tournaments like Kuksu, each player has three hours base time, and five 1-minute countdowns for the overtime period. New tournaments with modern titles such as "Championship" or "Baduk King" may have shorter thinking time like less than an hour each with 30 or 40 second countdowns.

The game[1] involved endless reading of variations and counting of territories. I was slightly behind by the time we were getting into the endgame, but luckily my opponent made a few mistakes due to time pressure. Through the mess, I managed to gain a few points, and eventually won the game by a half point. I knew I won the game by a half point when the game was almost at the end, and I felt relieved and excited at the same time.

Today's victory was especially meaningful for the following reasons:

1. The top four players receive seats in next year's main tournament without going through the preliminary round.

2. With one more win, I will be the finalist for the best-of-three match for the first time in my life.

3. It was the last main tournament of the year that I wasn't eliminated from yet. So, I wanted to stay in the tournament as long as I could.

Another thing about this tournament is that I have told my boss that I was resigning from my job as of December 31st, but I decided to move to Daejeon after this tournament is over. So, in January and

---

[1]Appendix: ○ Lee Jihyun – Lee Hajin ●

February if I am still in the running in this tournament, my life will be like the pre-work days when I spent most of my days studying baduk.

## Why Art?

DECEMBER 6<sup>TH</sup> 2008 — When you work five days a week, the weekends are so sweet that they just disappear like a chocolate ice cream you just bought. Still, what can I do other than make the most of what I get?

It must have snowed throughout last night, as if the sky knew Saturdays must look special. Though my place has a few problems, it has a decent view from the window. This morning, I was looking out the window and thought the view covered with snow was like a Go board where black didn't play at all. Haha, baduk player, aren't I?

In the afternoon, I went to the Seoul National Museum of Arts to see the special exhibition from "Centre Pompidou." Pompidou is a complex culture center in Paris, and they are known to have a great collection of art. I saw an ad for this exhibition in a newspaper one day, and was intrigued by the names of Picasso, Chagall, and Miro. I wanted to see what the exhibition had, and finally took the chance today.

On my way to the museum, I couldn't help thinking about the conversation I had a few days ago with Won, a friend of mine. I told him that I was thrilled to go see the exhibition, and he asked the following questions that no one asked me before.

Won: Why do you like seeing art?

Me: I feel moved when I see it.

Won: Why are you moved?

Me: Umm......

Won: What qualities of art do you think move you?

Me: Umm......

Well, I didn't really know what to say. I never thought about it seriously. I became interested in art when I was 12 years old. I was living at my teacher's house with fellow students who also aspired to be professional players. We had limited free time, and even more limited options as in what to do with it. So, what we usually did was read books. In the morning before breakfast, on a bus to the school, after lunch, or before going to bed. Whenever I had more than 10 minutes of free time, I would just open a book and start reading it. My favorite genre was classical literature such as *Jane Eyre* and *Oliver Twist,* but I would also read other books like *Sherlock Holmes* or *The Chronicles of Narnia.*

One day, I found this book called, *The Woman Who Reads Paintings.* It was a collection of essays that one female artist wrote about her own pieces and other famous ones. The book had a lot of pictures of different artwork, as well as interesting stories about herself. It wasn't the kind of a book that I would expect to find interesting, but somehow I felt compelled to buy it. Then, I liked the book so much that I must have read it like a dozen times. Sometimes, I would open a random page and just stare at a picture of a great artist's masterpiece.

Coming back to the exhibition today, I must admit my disappointment. The ticket was not cheap, and they had only two pieces of Chagall. Although it's hard to say which artist is my favorite, Chagall is definitely in the top five. His pieces are enchanting and inspiring, and they feel like pieces of my dreams. You know, dreams don't make much sense when I try to recall them, but there are fragments and images in corners of my mind. Yet, I don't regret going to the exhibition because you really can't expect a lot more in Korea. Just one lesson for the next time was that I should find someone to accompany me. Sharing my thoughts about the art would have been more interesting than keeping them all to myself.

Also, I came up with the following reasons why I like art, going through the exhibition today :

1. I can see history: People, buildings, fashion, trends, culture, and wars as well as ways of thinking and philosophy.

2. It inspires me with various colors, styles and techniques.

3. Everyone interprets and perceives differently even if they are looking at the same piece, and it shows us other ways of seeing things.

4. It is a good way to broaden your general knowledge and improve your artistic sense. Also it sometimes helps you start conversations with others.

## One Typical Day

DECEMBER 8ᵀᴴ 2008 — It's interesting how I felt my routine life would last forever. It felt that way when I was studying baduk, but it certainly changed when I became pro. My lifestyle as a new pro was relatively typical with study groups, tournaments, and social gatherings. I would see many pros who had been living just like that for 10 or more years. Yet, I had to change my lifestyle again when my dad's company went bankrupt. It's been about two years since I started working at YBA, and now that I can almost carry out my daily routine blindfolded, it's about to change again.

So let me summarize my day today, which would've been a quite typical day for the last two years. I don't think I like this life particularly well, but I will miss it from time to time as it fades away slowly from my memory. Life is just like that, I think. No matter good or bad, memories are memories, and you miss them once they become dusty in your mind. So, here it is, what my typical day looks like!

7:00 a.m.

Opened my eyes and stretched out for my phone to turn off the alarm. Spent some time tumbling about in my bed. At last I forced myself to get out of bed and turned on the light. It was still dark outside. Had some bread and orange juice, and got ready to go to work.

8:00 a.m.

Left home on time and walked to the subway station. Wanted to buy a newspaper, but I missed the chance because the train arrived as soon as I did. It takes over an hour by subway to get to YBA, and I buy newspapers once or twice a week. Today I read my book instead. These days I am reading *Invisible Man* by Ralph Ellison, which I got as a gift from Jon, a kind and friendly Go player from Seattle. The book is interesting, but also depressing. Arriving at the station, I bought a cappuccino before entering the office, to celebrate Monday.

9:30 a.m.

I started work by checking emails. Not all my emails are relevant to my "work" though, so don't tell my boss about it. Then, I made several diagrams and brief commentaries to send to the baduk weekly newspaper. (I do this every week.) Then, I moved on to my main work. I am an in-house textbook author. That is, I plan, design, and write baduk books for the students at YBA. Topics of the books vary. For instance, I finished a series of opening books last week, and now I am working on a series of life and death problem books. As I mentioned before, these days I am also teaching Alexa and Javier from 11:30 to 12:30.

12:30 p.m.

The lunch break is an hour. I went to a small restaurant just across the street with my coworkers and had kimchi fried rice. Then, I came back to the office right away to surf the Internet for a while.

1:30 p.m.

I'm often distracted in the morning by other tasks, but I spend most of my afternoon hours focused on the books. In my team, there are three people: My boss, me, and the book designer, and we sometimes have a pro player work as a freelancer. This is how it usually works: my boss decides on a topic and the difficulty level of the next book. Then, I plan what to include in what order. When my boss approves, I discuss it with the designer, and she makes the layout and template for the book. Then, I make the diagrams, write the explanations, put them into the template, and save them with the page number.

6:00 p.m.

Time to go home! Though I had a good lunch, I was really hungry again, so I went out with a few pros who either study or teach at YBA, and we had Korean-style hot noodles for dinner.

8:30 p.m.

Got home and turned on my laptop. I usually spend the evening surfing the Internet, reading books, writing my blog, or watching movies. I know I am mostly sitting all day and it would be a good idea to do something more active, but I feel tired after work. Well, something to think about, though. Then I go to bed at about midnight. That's now!

Good night!

## My Teacher's Birthday

DECEMBER 14TH 2008 — It's my baduk teacher's birthday today. His name is Cha Soo-kwon and he is a professional 7 dan, who runs a baduk academy north of Seoul. As I mentioned previously, I started at his academy when I was 9 years old. Although I was still young, it was a critical time to get serious if I wanted to pursue Go as a career. The academy was about two hours by car from home, and I moved to my teacher's house to live with his family and other students. I became a pro at 16, yet I stayed there until I was 19, at which point I got my own place in Seoul to be independent. Living at his house for about 10 years, I feel connected to my teacher far beyond a typical teacher-student relationship.

In order to celebrate our teacher's birthday, my baduk classmates and I agreed to visit him together today. Because my place is in the eastern part of Seoul, I had to go across town and it took me about an hour and a half by subway to get there. On my way, I remembered the days I took this subway line to play in my Insei league games. All the emotions – and a lot of books!

During the last few days, I thought about what to prepare for his birthday, but I couldn't decide until the last minute. It was clear that the wrong gift could backfire, because he wouldn't be happy to receive anything expensive from me. So I ended up getting a big chocolate cake for all of us to share. Trust me, it was not just because I like chocolate, my teacher likes it too.

I was the last person to arrive at the academy and everyone was already talking in a group. I was really happy to see them again, and it felt as if it had been only a few days since I last saw them. Also I got to see some of my juniors for the first time. They were adorable and seemed happily surprised by our sudden appearance.

Soon it was lunch time and we all went to a traditional Korean restaurant where we used to go for special occasions. Over lunch, we talked about his new students at the academy, baduk community, and our future plans. My teacher was against my decision to move to Daejeon because he thinks staying in Seoul is important for my tournament career. Yet, at least he agreed that it would be nice for me to live with my family again. I suppose you just can't have it all. Then the conversation moved on, and my teacher and his wife began telling us about the qualities of good husbands. Their main point was that we shouldn't be won over by superficial things, and they must have the right vision and discipline. So, I told them that I was usually attracted to smart men. They replied it was also important, but it shouldn't be my top priority because some men use their brightness in the wrong way. They added that they knew some decent young men. So if I wanted, probably a few years later, they would be happy to introduce me. You know, I am just 20 years old now, and I found it rather amusing that they were already concerned about my marriage.

With my teacher, though, I could really talk about anything. He was different from all the other baduk teachers in Korea. For one thing, most teachers, prodigies, and their parents shared the belief that you needed to sacrifice your general education entirely in order to succeed in baduk, and when the prodigies become professional players, their lack of other education won't matter as much since they already have a professional career. Thus, it was typical for my rivals to skip half of their classes in elementary school, and most of their classes in middle school and up. My teacher disagrees. He thinks it's important to have at least some general education, so we attended most classes in elementary school, and about two-thirds of our middle school classes.

For another, my teacher loves anything close to nature. He would take us to mountains for hiking as often as he could, he taught us the tea ceremony and shared his various tea selections, or sometimes suggested an impromptu trip to the southern countryside where we would find a beautiful river and relaxing scenery. Moreover, he would encourage us to read books outside baduk. This is all quite different from any other baduk academy, and I love my teacher for it.

After lunch, I stayed there a few more hours, and came back home before dinner time. Although we all wanted to stay longer, my teacher had other students to teach and take care of. I don't know yet when I will be visiting him again, but hopefully it will be in the near future.

## Last Lesson

December 22$^{\text{ND}}$ 2008 — *The Last Lesson* by Alphonse Daudet was a simple but powerful short story that made a strong impression on me. The main character of the story is a small boy who does not like to go to school. One day, he is again lingering on the way to school, finding everything else in the street more interesting. As he arrives at the school, he senses that something is different, and soon learns that it was the last lesson because his town just became German from

French. Can you guess why I am talking about this story? Well, I had a similar experience today.

I have been attending Spanish class on Sundays for about half a year now. When I say this to people, the first question is "Why?" In Korea, you study English, Chinese, or Japanese. Especially in the baduk community, Chinese and Japanese are the most popular languages to study because we have frequent interactions with Chinese and Japanese players. So, why did I choose Spanish? For one thing, it seemed like a fun language to study, but mostly I wanted to differentiate myself from other baduk players. This is secret, though – I usually say only the first half to people who ask this question.

We have a small class here, often only one or two students attend. I am not sure how many students were registered, but probably fewer than five. As I said, Spanish is not popular, and Sunday morning is not quite an attractive time to study either. Anyway, throughout the last six months of these intense lessons, thanks to the small class size, I became close with my teacher on a personal level. Our class was from 9:30 a.m. to noon, and he would ask me to come along for lunch after the class, or send me latin pop songs via email.

I came to the Spanish class on time, and received a text from him. "Sorry, I am running late. Be there in 5 minutes." It's not his first time to come a bit late, so it never bothered me. After all, it's Sunday, and I respect him for being an amazing Spanish teacher. I even imagine he is the best Spanish teacher in Korea, though to be fair I don't know any other Spanish teachers.

Anyway, he walked into the class soon enough, and we covered two past tenses: "imperfecto" and "indefinido". These were confusing, especially when it came to irregular verbs. After the three-and-a-half-hour long class, way longer than usual, he announced that it was the last lesson. He had got a job offer from Hyundai Engineering to work in Equatorial Guinea as a Spanish translator and writer. Apparently this is the only African country that uses Spanish and it takes 34 hours to get there from Korea. At this sudden news, I felt like crying but tried to keep calm. I didn't really want to make the atmosphere awkward. So, instead of being sad, I asked him if I could visit him one day, and he said I would always be welcome.

It's hard for me to imagine what it would be like to live in Guinea. Summer is my favorite season, but I am not sure if I want to live in summer all year round. Also, the things I take for granted, such as electricity, the Internet, or public transportation might not be available everywhere. Yet, I would have made the same choice if I were my Spanish teacher. This is going to be a once in a lifetime experience, and I am happy for him. For now, I am moving back to Daejeon to live with my family, but someday I also want to live abroad, to have my own adventures.

## Farewell Lunch

DECEMBER 31ST 2008 — Today is the last day of the year, and also my last day at YBA. From the subway ride in the morning, my mind was full of mixed emotions. I told myself that I should behave just as I would on any other day, but the self-spell didn't seem to be working. So I got a cappuccino before entering the office as a calming device for my stirred mind.

I decided to move to Daejeon about a month ago and immediately brought the news to my boss. My boss is a professional 7 dan, and I had been working with him for two years now. He was disappointed to learn that I was leaving so soon. I knew he was not just pretending, because he hadn't been shy about letting me know that he valued me. He would often speak highly of me to other people, things like, "Hajin's such a talented girl in many ways. I wonder why these young men are not asking her out when she is single." At first he tried to convince me to stay. He couldn't insist, though, when I told him that I had been away from my home for 12 years and wanted to live with my family again.

There is a more or less typical lifecycle of professional players in Korea. One would become a pro somewhere between 15 and 21 years old. Then, you would focus on your tournament career until around 30 to 35. When I say "focus", I mean playing in tournaments would be your main (or only) source of income. Other than playing matches, young pros would study baduk, exercise, learn a foreign language, or pursue any number of hobbies. When one gets older than 30, and one's performance is trending downward, one might start a new career in other areas such as teaching, TV commentary, getting a job in baduk-related fields, and so on. If possible, you would still play in tournaments, but at this point you would rely more on income from other activities.

My case was unusual, because I needed to support my family financially. My boss learned about my situation through my friend, and he kindly offered me this job. For the last two years I've been supporting my family with my prize money from tournaments, and my own life in Seoul with my salary. Sometimes I felt jealous that my pro friends could enjoy their lives while saving most of their tournament income. Seeing my family recovering from the bottom, though, was worth more than anything in the world.

Coming back to the story of my day today, my boss had arranged a farewell lunch for me. In attendance were my boss, two colleagues of mine, and me. My two colleagues are not pros, but are both double-digit kyu players. One of them does the art and graphic design for our books, and the other takes care of financial and administrative matters for YBA. Usually we go to a nearby cafeteria for lunch where we could have a reasonable meal for a low price. Today, my boss didn't tell us where we were going, and it turned out he reserved a table at a fancy steak house. I was very touched. Not that the price of the food is important, but it just showed that he cares about me.

Over lunch, we talked about the last two years. In the beginning we created online content such as video lectures and study materials. Then, we moved on to in-house textbooks, covering openings, joseki, life and death problems, top players' game collections, beginners' books and so on. Special memories from summer camps with hundreds of students, dinner meetings, or birthday parties were also fun topics to talk about. Although I often wished I didn't have to work, I felt a bit sad to think it was my last day at YBA.

Tomorrow, I am going to Daejeon to celebrate new year's day with my family, and probably stay there for a few days. Then, I will come back to Seoul to study baduk until my semi-final match. Yes, it seems like I am going back to the typical life of a young pro!

## New Year's Resolutions

JANUARY 5TH 2009 — I had a relaxing holiday at home over new years, and came back to Seoul yesterday. How strange it feels to be free during weekdays! My top priority should be studying baduk, but I am still thrilled about all the the free time I have now. It's a lucky coincidence that I am having this turning point of my life just as the new year comes, since it's the perfect time to review the last year and draft my new year's resolutions.

Looking back the year 2008, I am proud of the following eight events:

- Won a minor tournament called "Ju-Jak-wang." Literally, Ju-jak is a symbolic name meaning "phoenix", and Wang means "king". It's not a major title, but most female pro players participated, including all the top ones.

- Won a bronze medal at the 2008 World Mind Sports Games in Beijing.

- Won 10 official matches in a row for the first time in my professional career.

- Took violin and Spanish classes.

- Travelled around the West Coast of the US.

- Worked at YBA as a textbook writer.

- Started an English blog.

Here are my New Year's resolutions for 2009!

- Play in the final round of a major title (and even better would be getting the title, haha).

- Write blog entries.

- Improve my English.

- Continue my Spanish and violin lessons.

- Take the TOEFL and the SAT.

- Attend the US Go Congress in Washington DC.

- Exercise (in any form).

- Read five books per month (or 60 books a year).

Looking at these two lists, I can't help realizing how much my life has changed since I became pro. For so long, my new year's resolution was always the same: "Study baduk hard and become a stronger player." Or "Study baduk hard and pass the pro qualification." As you can see, I didn't have much of a life outside the baduk board. Yet it didn't mean baduk was my only interest. I constantly felt curious about many other things, but the doors to them were never open. The conversations would go like this:

"Mom, I want to learn music. What if I take piano lessons?"

"Honey, you need to focus on baduk. You realize how hard it is to become pro, right?"

"Mom, can I learn tennis?"

"I understand you want to try new things. You can try anything you want once you become pro, but not before. You should focus now."

"Mom, someone asked me out, and I think he is nice. Can I have a boyfriend?"

"Um… I don't think this is good time. Why don't you wait until you become pro?"

So, guess what? I became pro, and I picked up so many new subjects like English, yoga, violin, Spanish, table tennis, a boyfriend, and so on. Although it turned out not all of them were my thing, I still had meaningful experiences trying each of them. Also, at some point in the future, I still want to learn swimming, tennis, and Latin dancing!

There are professional players, usually the top pros, who do not find anything interesting outside baduk. I wonder if my insatiable curiosity towards the wider world means I am not top player material. Yet, even if that is the case, I will still choose to be me because I am happy with myself.

## Final Round

JANUARY 22ND 2009 — YES! I DID IT! I still can't believe that I won today! It was a semi-final match, and today's win[2] meant I got a ticket to the best-of-three final for the women's Kuksu title! For one thing, I will be playing this big match against Rui Naiwei 9p, the living legend of all female players. In addition, all title matches are played in the special room in the KBA building. This is a fancy room with one board and two big arm chairs, reserved for titles or final matches. I've never had a chance to play there before, and now my dream will come true!

---

[2] Appendix: ○ Lee Hajin – Lee Minjin ●

When I was studying to become pro, I would see this room in pictures. In the pictures were usually Lee Changho 9p, Cho Hunhyun 9p, and other top players in Korea. Even though they were mere pictures, I could feel the tension and serenity in the atmosphere. I first entered the room right after I became pro. As a part of the training program, new pros were required to take a number of game-recording jobs. This is a one-day task of recording a professional game on two paper sheets, as well as recording how much time was spent on each move using a stopwatch. The job also includes doing the countdown using the same stopwatch. Luckily, one of the games I recorded was a title match, and I got to sit in the room for a day. Yet you know, it's just not the same. Though I was happy to witness what it was like to have a game there, I couldn't help thinking that one day I would come back as one of the two competitors.

I have been preparing for today's match since I came back from Daejeon, putting off a number of things such as studying English or Spanish. I even disappointed my friend. Just a few days ago, one friend of mine invited me for a movie because he got two tickets. You know, I wouldn't say no to a free movie, but I had this big match coming up. So, I said "no" like a responsible pro player. Anyway, I tried to focus on studying baduk, and when I wasn't studying, I read a book. Because of my long-time habit of filling all non-baduk time with books, reading comforts me like nothing else.

Anyway, I am thrilled and excited about making it to the best-of-three final match, and I should work harder to win the title!

# Group Study

MARCH 5<sup>TH</sup> 2009 — I have bad news: I lost the first game[3] in the best-of-three final match about two weeks ago. I was so depressed about the game that I didn't want to write a blog entry for a while.

---

[3] Appendix: ○ Lee Hajin – Rui Naiwei ●

Oh well. Now I am feeling better, and I have my second game in four days, next Monday. This time I will be playing with black, so maybe I will have a better game. Usually I have no preference between black or white, but my opponent, Rui Naiwei 9p, is a lot stronger with black then white. Also, one advantage of having black is that you can prepare your opening in advance.

Today I went to a group study. Professional players like to study in groups because it is a chance to get different perspectives. There are several professional study groups in Seoul, and these groups also form social circles as they not only study, but also have lunch, dinner, or hang out together. I am a member of a study group called "Guro." which is named after the neighborhood our study room is located. Our group meets every Thursday, and we have eight members including me; Paek Daehyun 6p, Ryoo Jaehyoung 8p, An Joyoung 9p, Lee Hyunwook 6p, Lee Heesung 7p, Park Jieun 9p, and Lee Jihyeon 3p. And, I am the youngest one there.

The group study starts at 10 o'clock in the morning. If anyone comes late, they have to pay a penalty of 10,000 KRW. Once in a while we buy snacks and fruit to share among members with the collected money from the late fee. Common study materials are the latest top players' games. We would discuss openings, the results of certain local battles, (who is better here? Would you take black or white?), other possible moves (what happens if black plays here instead of this?), and endgame sequences. After playing through the big games, we would also go over our own matches. Do you think pros play flawlessly? You should come here and see how a pro can be scolded. ("WHAT? YOU PLAYED THERE?!?")

Today, we specifically studied opening variations for black, because I promised to buy dinner for everyone if I win the next title match. I was joking, but my group would have done the same even if I didn't make that offer.

I lost confidence after the first game because it was such a one-sided game. I was white and I felt like I never had a chance all along.

Yet, today's study group made me feel much better about the upcoming match, and I will try to make my group proud.


# The End

MARCH 10TH 2009 — It was the biggest stage I've ever played on. I had dreamed about playing this exact match my entire life. In a way, I realized my dream since I did play the match. I just didn't win. I lost the second match[4] yesterday, and lost the Kuksu title match, 2-0. The result is not everything, though. At least I gained this priceless experience. So I should be grateful.

But, it was still painful. So painful that it made my heart sick. In order to distract myself, I talked with a friend on the phone for a long time and watched two romantic comedies, with beer. It was a long night.

When I was young, I was afraid of being punished. I know no one likes to be punished, but I was a bit extreme. I just couldn't stand the painful moment, and would do anything to prevent the situation. In baduk, however, you don't always have the control over your results. It's not like you can win just because you are determined to win. On the contrary, I would often play worse, feeling the pressure that I had to win.

There was a time that we had to memorize 10 professional games a day as punishment if we failed to get certain results in tournaments. One day before a tournament, I was feeling nervous that I wouldn't meet the goal and would be punished. I must have looked so gloomy. My teacher came to me and asked if I was okay. I told him that I was really worried that I might not win enough games tomorrow. He said "If you come to me after the tournament and tell me you did your best and you don't regret anything, I will say nothing about it,

---

[4] Appendix: ○ Rui Naiwei – Lee Hajin ●

no punishment." I won four out of five games in the tournament, which was more than enough to avoid punishment.

I lost this title match and felt a thunderstorm inside, but now I am thinking about what my teacher told me 10 years ago. I gave it my best shot, so I should stop punishing myself.

## Professional Friendship

MARCH 24TH 2009 — I have two close friends, Sesil and Eunsun. They are both professional players and we were all born in the same year. We used to hang out almost every day when we were new pros, but I couldn't see them as much once I started working. Yet even when we meet for the first time in months, we are still so close and comfortable it's as if we had been seeing each other every day, just like the old days. We share life experiences, memories, as well as our secrets. Isn't it nice to talk with people to whom you don't have to explain things? For example, if I say, "I saw him again," they would say, "Oh, come on, get over him," instead of saying, "Who?" or "What about him?" Anyway, we still manage to meet up once in awhile, and we would go to a café and talk for hours and hours.

Not much different from any other friendship so far, right? Because we are all pros, however, we face each other in matches more often than you would guess. This is especially true for me because there are only about 30 female pros in Korea at the moment.

Today, I played against Eunsun at the final round of the preliminary tournament of the GGAuction Cup. The GGAuction Cup is a team competition between female players and senior male players over 45 years old, in a "win and continue" format. Each team has 12 players, and one player plays the other team's players until he or she loses. We both played on the women's team last year, but this time only today's winner would join the team.

I met her 10 minutes before the match, in the waiting room of the Baduk TV studio. We greeted each other cheerfully as usual, then said nothing. It was just a bit awkward. I thought about telling her about last weekend, but the time we had was kind of too short to start any meaningful conversation. Maybe she felt something similar as well. We moved to the playing room and started playing. Our game was very complicated and we were both in countdown. Eunsun had a few chances to kill my big group, but she missed them. Eventually, I won the game. We exchanged a few opinions, and I was called by the commentator to give a short winner's interview. When I got out of the studio, Eunsun was not there any more.

This was not the first time I had played against her, by the way. We'd had several games before, as well as several against Sesil. I believe it will always be awkward before or after the game, no matter how many times we play each other. When we meet again some time after a match, though, we are as happy as usual, just like all old friends. We are professional players, and we respect our matches and our friends. Yet, I can tell you this: When I play them, I feel slightly less glad to win and less sad to lose.

## Part II
# Different Worlds

## Mathematics

MARCH 27TH 2009 — I finally moved to my parents' place a few days ago. The kuksu title match was over, and I had no upcoming matches for a while. As my first project in Daejeon, I decided to catch up on mathematics, taking the opportunity of being at home with my dad and little sister, who are good at high-level math.

When I visited Europe three years ago, I noticed that most European players were either software engineers or mathematicians. This intrigued me, because there is no comparable pattern in Korean players. My theory was that most Korean people are familiar with baduk, and thus the game is accessible to all Koreans equally. In European countries, however, only a small percentage of people know about the game. So, it's unlikely to even hear about baduk, but there are two main channels where it's frequently mentioned. The first is that this is the only game where computers can't compete with strong human players, and the second is through the movie "A Beautiful Mind." Yet, my knowledge in either field is so limited that I can't tell whether there are more connections between Go players and computer or math experts.

For most Korean pros, computer science and mathematics are an unknown world. I learned to use a few basic applications at my work, but if it weren't for my job, I would still be using a computer only for emails and web browsing. In my defense, many pros are like that. Some of them wouldn't even have an email address. You might find it strange, but just imagine baduk players' lives. Since we were young, we lived with baduk sets and books. When we do use computers, it's often to play baduk online. Why would we ever need anything else? After all, we don't need to write a paper or make a presentation to play baduk.

Math is about the same. Studying baduk to become a pro takes up all your time, and it's just impossible to keep up with math classes at school. In fact, often baduk prodigies don't go to school at all. I also gave up on math early on, and it's become an alien language to me since then. I could do arithmetic calculations, but didn't know anything about algebra or geometry, for example. Humanities classes such as literature or history were better, thanks to my hobby of reading books. Now that I think about it, maybe I should have read more books about mathematics.

Today was my first day studying math, and I learned about "greatest common divisors" and "least common multiples." It was fun. My dad is helping me with my questions, since he studied Electronics Engineering and math in university. Aren't I lucky? I can't wait to study more difficult topics and discover all the similarities between baduk and math.

## A Match Against My Ex-Hero

APRIL 15$^{\text{TH}}$ 2009 — My life in Daejeon has been peaceful. I am studying mathematics, reading a lot of books, and taking squash lessons in the morning. Yet, this life would be a bit bland without matches. So, I was happy that a new tournament kicked off today.

There was the first round of LG Cup preliminary, and my opponent was Hu Yaoyu 8p. It was unbelievable that I met him – a $1/400$ chance. Hu Yaoyu 8p is one of the top Chinese players. He has calm and delicate style like Lee Changho and is good at keeping balance. Outside the board, he is kind of good looking and easy going. I used to be a big fan of his when I was younger, imagining him to be gentle and smart.

As a new pro, I volunteered a few times to record for international championships in order to be able to choose his games. You know, when I record, I not only get to see his game from the beginning to the end, but also see him immersed in the game for hours. One day, I got a chance to get on the same bus with him. It was on the way to the dinner place for all Korean and Chinese pros. On the bus, I asked a friend of mine, who is also a pro and can speak Chinese, to tell him that I was his fan! I was so embarrassed, but quickly became happy when Hu Yaoyu had a big smile and offered me a handshake. As time passed, I moved on, and I heard he got married a while ago.

LG Cup and Samsung Cup both have an open preliminary round, which means it is open to all professional players in the world. This was sensational at first, because the conventional way was to give a certain number of seats to each country for the main round. There are still country quotas in this system for the main round, but it's just more interesting to see the preliminary round with pro players from other countries as well. Another thing about this open preliminary is that it broke the unspoken rule which said you had to pay airfare, room and board, and offer some prize money to get professional players from other countries to attend. In this open preliminary, however, many Chinese and Japanese pro players would come to Korea at their own expense, and receive prize money depending on how they performed.

I arrived at the playing venue about 20 minutes before the match was to start. Already many pro players were around the hall, talking in groups. I said hi to a few friends, made myself some hot tea, and found my seat. I was feeling a bit tired after a disturbed sleep and an early train ride from Daejeon, but it wasn't significant and the hot tea was already refreshing me. Soon a group of Chinese pros walked in, and Hu Yaoyu was one of them. He found me sitting, gave me a slight nod, and walked away with the group. It is common for one player to sit right before the starting time when the other player is already sitting, especially if you have nothing to talk about.

I played a strong move in the early opening, and a complicated battle formed. The positions were in my favor, and I was actually leading the game! As the game advanced, though, he quietly caught up with me and the game became quite close. In the end I was slightly behind, and I fought back but eventually let my big group die. The game lasted about six hours, and we did some post game analysis for about an hour and a half. Though we didn't have a common language, him speaking only Chinese, the moves and gestures were adequate for our communication. Overall, it was such a memorable experience, even though I lost. Trust me, it's rare that I can feel good after losing, and this is one of the moments that I appreciate being a pro player myself.

## Baduk and School

APRIL 16^TH 2009 — These days I am researching universities in and outside Korea. It's been over a year since I graduated from high school, and I am interested in going to university. Although my career as a pro player doesn't require a university degree, I am curious about the world outside baduk and decided to apply for at least one school. Yet, it seems like my options are limited because most universities don't offer special points for admission even if you are a professional baduk player. I became pro before graduating from middle school, and I focused all my energy on pro tournaments throughout high school. I did well as a pro, but my grades in high school were always at the bottom.

This is a typical pattern for pros, and that's why very few pros go to a university. We spend our lifetime studying baduk, and we are both unwilling and afraid to leave tournaments. There are hundreds of students who are studying baduk to become professional players, but the Korea Baduk Association strictly limits the number of new pros each year. In order to succeed in this competitive system, most baduk prodigies sacrifice general education at school and spend the whole day at a baduk school. Some people, however, argue that we shouldn't be dismissing general education so much, especially at such an early age. My teacher shared this view as well, and thanks to that I attended my middle school part-time while my rivals were skipping their classes entirely.

It is difficult to say which is right or wrong. I personally agree with my teacher and I am grateful that I got to take all my classes in elementary school and some classes in middle school. I believe my baduk skills improved from school classes as well, and I didn't fall behind in baduk, even though I studied less than my rivals. However, none of the top pros in Korea took classes in schools since they were very young. Also, it is generally believed that being great in one specific area is better than being good in many fields. What I believe is that everyone's different and we should not force one model on all students.

Coming back to my university search, I seem to have two possibilities: The first one is to go to the US and study at a community college. If I do well, I can try to transfer to a state university after two years. The second option is to find a university in Korea with an admissions program for students with specific talents. For the moment I am not sure which one would be better for me, so I guess I will keep doing my research.

# GGAuction Camp

April 29th 2009 — In an earlier entry I talked about my match against Eunsun, my close friend. After winning the game, I joined the women's team in the GGAuction Cup. If you don't remember about the tournament, this is an annual team competition between female professional players and senior (over 45 years old) professional players. Each team has 12 players, and one player continues playing until they lose. This competition launched three years ago, and it quickly became popular among fans due to its rare qualities. This year, the sponsor planned a "one-night camp" as an opening ceremony, and I was invited to come along. At first I thought all players were invited, but it turned out only the first two players from each team were invited to attend the camp.

When I arrived at the KBA in the morning, a big bus was waiting for us. Next to the bus were boxes of beer, snacks, baduk sets, and all kinds of things. Though an important match was ahead of me, just looking at the bus and boxes made me feel excited as if I were going on a picnic. In fact, it could be only a picnic, if Miri, our first player, won her first game. Anyway, we got on the bus with a few KBA staff members, journalists, and about a dozen lucky baduk fans, who won a draw among over 300 applicants.

Our destination was a small resort called 'GG Valley'. The resort has about 10 cottages, the main building where you can play baduk, a cafeteria, and it's completely surrounded by nature. Along the resort, you could see a stream of water flowing downward. GG Valley is GGAuction's employees' retreat place as well as a vacation destination for families. The place is located in Gangwon Province, by Mt. Yoo-myoung. It took us about an hour and a half to get there from Seoul. The scenery was beautiful, the air was fresh and the weather was perfect with warm sunlight and cool breeze.

We unpacked and took a break, and had lunch at the cafeteria building. There were a number of ladies who prepared traditional Korean cuisine for us. The vegetables and grains were all fresh and tasty. After lunch, I had a short walk with Miri. Miri became pro just last year, and agreed to be our first player. She said it was the first tournament where she'd passed the preliminary matches, so this was her first match in any main round, and she seemed quite nervous. The first player from the Senior team was Cha Minsoo professional

4-dan, who is well known by his English name, Jimmy Cha. Mr. Cha has such an interesting life story that there was a novel and a TV show about him in Korea. Anyway, he is more famous as a poker player than a baduk player, and that's what I told Miri. I knew he was still quite sharp, but I did my part to support my teammate!

During the first match I analyzed the game by myself in the public commentary room.

Maybe out of anxiety, Miri overplayed in the opening, and it seemed hopeless for her until Mr. Cha made a big mistake under countdown pressure and the game became quite difficult for both. The ko fight in the upper-left was the crucial point, but Miri misjudged the situation and chose a safe way, which was not enough to win the game.

As she lost, it became my turn to play Mr. Cha. I learned about him when I was 15 from the TV show I mentioned. It was called "All In", and was based on his life story. This TV show was extremely popular in Korea, having the elements of poker, gang fights, gambling, romance, casinos, and so on. You might assume that he was an old player past his prime, but in the previous edition of this team competition, he brought five wins to the senior team. When I realized that I would play him, I was both thrilled and worried at the same time. You know, I was curious to see what it would be like to play him, but I was also afraid that I would lose. I wanted to contribute to my team by winning at least one game!

My impression was that he was good at navigating complicated situations. So, I thought I would play calmly this time, but a big fight appeared[5] in the opening, as usual for me. Fortunately I managed to settle the big fight in my favor in the middle game, and after that I just had to play safe to maintain my advantage. It felt so good to win. Cameras followed me asking for interviews and pictures, and the baduk fans there congratulated me as I walked out of the playing room.

---

[5] Appendix: ○ Jimmy Cha – Lee Hajin ●

After the match, I felt exhausted and hungry. When the cameras were done with me, I quietly went back to the room and stayed there until dinner time came. Our dinner was an amazing garden barbecue party! They set up several tables and barbecue barrels and coals, with plenty of vegetables and beer to go with the meat. Not only one kind of meat, but they had pork, chicken, sausages on the grill. Over the dinner, I had such a pleasant time with baduk fans, baduk TV staff members and some journalists. It was so nice! I think this kind of camp was a new thing for a professional tournament, and I hope it marks the start of bringing variety to the conservative style of professional events.

## Baduk TV

MAY 12TH 2009 — Coming back from the GGAuction Camp, the tournament continued at the Baduk TV Studio, two games per week. I won the next match, but lost my 3rd game by one-and-a-half points. I was disappointed that I was already out of the tournament, but I suppose two wins was not a bad result. Now I will have to root for my team members.

I had another occasion to visit the Baduk TV studio today. For your information, Baduk TV is a cable TV channel that broadcasts baduk 24/7. Their programs include professional and amateur tournaments, lectures, news, and so on. You may be surprised that there is such demand, but actually Baduk TV has a large viewership among cable channels in Korea. In prime time, it's the third most popular, after a movie channel and a kids' channel. Plus, there is another TV channel that only broadcasts baduk on satellite TV.

Anyway, I made my debut on Baduk TV as a commentator today, though it was kind of a one-time-only deal. Since I was young, I somehow believed that I would always be a player, but never thought I would be a commentator. I was shy with cameras and wasn't confident in my looks. You know, TV people are glamorous and beautiful.

Yet, I received a special request, and I accepted the work both for the experience and for my late teacher.

For about two years starting from when I was 10 years old, we had Mr. Jeong, a professional 6-dan teacher at our baduk academy. He would have been with us for much longer, if it weren't for a car accident that took him from us. He was strict and a bit scary during study hours, but couldn't be more friendly once we were outside the classroom. He was like our uncle. He would play with us, and sometimes buy us ice cream. We were all devastated by the news of his terrible accident.

Mr. Jeong's family decided to host a children's baduk tournament to honor his passion for teaching. To support this cause, the KBA provided the playing venue without charge, many pro players volunteered to be referees of the tournament, Baduk TV also offered to broadcast the final round.

Years have passed since its beginning, and this year was already the 9th Jeong Hyunsan Cup. I was only a small girl then, but now I am a grown-up professional player. I was really glad that Baduk TV gave me the opportunity to contribute to the tournament and accepted the work without hesitation. I was afraid of cameras and had no experience with TV commentary, but I wanted to do this. Though the focus would be the commentary on the game, I was also happy to tell the world what a great teacher he was.

Baduk TV has a team of stylists, and they usually bring some clothes for commentators. What they brought for me was a girly yellow blouse and a black skirt. Something I wouldn't wear normally. Then, they did full make-up and hair styling on me for about an hour. It was my first time receiving such care, and I couldn't believe how totally different I looked. Well, in a good way, of course.

My commentary partner was a computer game commentator who had never done a baduk program before. He said he was 3-kyu when he was a child, but it turned out his memory of baduk was rather blurry. Sometimes he would misunderstand my explanations and make me embarrassed. Yet, I liked that he was willing to learn and had such a positive attitude.

The two hours' recording felt like 20 hours. So much light and heat inside the studio exhausted me. At some point I and my partner wondered if we would ever finish this thing, saying "can we go home today?" as a joke. There were a lot of re-takes, and repetitions for better footage. We all worked together, though, and managed to finish it! I am not sure if I liked commenting on TV or if I would try it again sometime, but it was definitely a memorable experience!

# Baduk and Regulations

MAY 23$^{RD}$ 2009 — I read an interesting article today about a dress code proposal for professional tournaments. The Korea Baduk Association (KBA) has no written rules about dress codes, but as a young pro, you can get scolded by senior pros if you wear something too casual for an official match. It is an unspoken rule that you should wear at least semi-formal attire, and I believe Japanese pros have a similar culture. Yet, there were several Chinese pro players who came to international matches in exercise clothes in the last few years, and that's what triggered the dress code proposal.

Now that I think about it, baduk competitions have few regulations but many unstated expectations. For one, you are allowed to leave your seat as many times as you want and as long as your time limit allows. It's bad manners to use your phone, but it is not prohibited. You only need to keep it in silent mode. Eating food during your game is considered impolite, but there is no regulation on that either.

We do have a few more regulations than we did in the early days, though. For example, smoking is not allowed in the playing venue. If your phone rings or you make distracting sounds with any of your belongings, you get a warning the first time, a two point penalty the second time, and forfeit the game on the third time.

Also, LG Cup introduced a new rule a couple years ago. Players cannot stay in the playing room during the lunch hour, and the room is locked until 10 minutes before resuming the game. In professional matches, it was an expectation that pro players should not discuss their games with other pros during the one-hour lunch break, but some Korean pros believed that young Chinese pros discussed their games together. Several Korean pros speak Chinese, and they said that they actually heard these things. It quickly became a hot topic, and now we have a new rule.

Though some people find it sad that we have to state obvious things, I believe it's a natural process as baduk is transitioning from a culture to a sport. As we continue in this direction, we might also see other sports problems such as illegal betting and doping, especially with big prize money and fame for winners. Yet, I believe these are problems we are willing to fight, if they come with more baduk fans around the world.

# 21,000 Hours

JUNE 2ND 2009 — My performance in tournaments hasn't been very satisfying since losing the final of the women's Kuksu title. I won two games in the GGAuction Cup, but that was about it. I am a bit discouraged, but somehow not as much as I would have been a few years ago. Being a professional player is wonderful, but I don't want to limit my life to the baduk world. As a pro player I feel like there isn't much I haven't se When I say this, though, many people, including my parents have difficulty sharing my view. They say it would be a pity not to use my baduk skills after putting so much time into gaining them. So, one day I did a rough calculation to see how many hours I had spent in baduk to become a pro.

I learned this game when I was 5 years old. In the beginning I studied one hour a day, five days a week at a private baduk academy, and I would play a few games with my parents on weekends. As I got older, one hour became two hours and then three hours a day, and I would play in local tournaments on the weekends. At the age of 9, I moved to a professional baduk academy over 200 kilometers away from home and lived at my teacher's house.

Living at my teacher's house with my fellow students, I would study baduk from 2 p.m. to 10 p.m. during school days, and 9 a.m. to 9 p.m. on school vacations. The daily routine would be a mix of studying books, playing internal league games, getting game reviews from the teacher, and playing online with random strong players. On weekends, we had tournaments or insei leagues (the Korea Baduk Association's official training program for young aspiring professional players) to play, and after coming back to the house we were required to record and review our games.

I passed the pro qualification at 16, about 11 years after I started playing. On average, my study hours looked like this:

- Age 5-6: $225\frac{\text{days}}{\text{year}} \times 1\frac{\text{hour}}{\text{day}} = 225$ hours

- Age 7-8: $250\frac{\text{days}}{\text{year}} \times 2 \text{ years} \times 2\frac{\text{hours}}{\text{day}} = 1,000$ hours

- Age 9-11: $275\frac{\text{days}}{\text{year}} \times 3 \text{ years} \times 7\frac{\text{hours}}{\text{day}} = 5,775$ hours

- Age 12-16: $300\frac{\text{days}}{\text{year}} \times 5 \text{ years} \times 8\frac{\text{hours}}{\text{day}} = 12,000$ hours

So, I could say I put about 21,000 hours into becoming a pro. Yet, I don't believe that these hours would wasted if I were to explore the world outside tournament play. It might take me some time to catch up with others who studied more in school, but when we are all learning something new, I am confident that I will be able to follow as well as anyone else.

# Daejeon Mayor's Cup

JUNE 13<sup>TH</sup> 2009 — The weather's been very nice, and I am enjoying a peaceful life in Daejeon with my family. I take squash lessons in the morning, study mathematics, read books at a café, and sometimes hang out with my family. Then, once in awhile I go to Seoul for a match or something. Today, however, I had a special activity as a professional player.

There are hundreds of amateur baduk events in Korea each year. I also used to compete in amateur tournaments, especially those for youth or female players. Yet, since I am now a professional player, I was invited to come to the Daejeon Mayor's Cup national amateur baduk championship today as a guest. It felt so strange to see young students sitting before boards, looking nervous, determined, or excited. When I was in these tournaments as a participant, I usually had high expectations for myself, and I would often experience indigestion and nausea from the stress. As a guest, now I sit on the stage with other VIPs, with no reason to tense up.

The differences began much earlier than this, actually. I got up early this morning and put on make-up, dressed up and wore high heels. Since many children were going to see me as a 'role model' I wanted to look nice and professional. When I was a player, I wouldn't care what I wore to the tournament. Maybe something comfortable, I guess. There was no awkward conversation at the breakfast table either. Before, there were questions like, "how do you feel today? are you ready for the tournament?" Instead, it's all now, "you look great today. Be nice to the kids, and don't forget to smile when you take pictures with them."

I paid no attention to opening ceremonies when I was a young participant at these tournaments. They were always the same. Some important guests would be introduced, a few of them would come out to the stage to deliver short speeches, and so on. Expecting most children to have a similar reaction, I felt both sad and relieved at the same time. I was sad that my presence here was probably not as significant as it may have seemed, but I was also relieved that it meant even if I did something terrible by accident, not all of the 500 participants would notice. Anyway, we had a very conventional opening ceremony, just as I expected, and all participants were instructed to start their games soon after.

When I was a player, I would wonder where the VIPs went after the opening ceremony and what they did behind the scenes. We were all guided down off the stage and to the VIP lounge. There were fancy leather chairs and tea tables set up, and as we walked in some tea, pastries, and fruit were served. I waited until all other guests were seated, then found my spot in the corner. In Korean society, your age matters a lot, and you are pretty much at the bottom of the hierarchy if you are 20 years old.

My simultaneous games began at 3 p.m. This was the latest time the organizers could start while making sure that all events were concluded before the closing ceremony at 5:30 p.m. By this time the high rankers were playing for medals, while the majority of the participants were eliminated. In this way, they have the maximum number of players eligible for simul games, without delaying the closing ceremony. When I was a new pro, I didn't like playing simultaneous games because it was so tiring. It was exhausting to play so many games at once, to play for hours walking around, and sometimes my back would hurt if the tables were too low. Yet, I changed my mind after Lee Minjin 5p once told me this: "I always do my best when I play simul games even if I don't feel up to it. It's one of many events for me, and though I might forget them soon enough, for some of the amateurs it will be a once in a lifetime event and they won't forget their game with a professional player. I really shouldn't ruin such a special thing." Can you imagine how much I was moved by this statement and influenced by it afterwards?

I also played several simul games when I was a child. At the time I thought we were all supposed to win, because I usually won against the pro players. It was much later that I learned it was actually the opposite. Now I play simul games on the pro side, and I rarely lose at all. I don't remember how I won as a child, but I guess either I had too many handicap stones or the pros wanted to encourage me to study harder. Today, I managed to win all eight boards in my simul games. You know, I am not nice enough to let small children win to encourage them. If they want to win, they have to earn it.

# Best Birthday

JUNE 21ST 2009 — It is my 21st birthday today! I guess I am officially a grown-up now. Although I haven't achieved anything "great" yet, I somehow feel proud of myself. Look! I am 21 years old!

Several days ago, my parents asked me what I wished for my birthday gift. I wanted to have a better violin, and my laptop was getting old. Some new clothes would be nice, too. Yet, none of them sounded special. My violin and laptop were still usable, and I don't care much for fashion anyway. Then, I asked myself what made me happier than anything else. Once the question was there, my answer came easily.

I love bookstores, and there is no place more exciting. I would walk around, read some pages of interesting looking ones, forgetting how time is flying by. Realizing this, I told my parents, "Would you take me to the largest bookstore in town and give me a few hours to pick out some books for my gift?"

My parents dropped me at a huge bookstore yesterday and told me I could stay as long as I wanted and choose as many books as I liked. Of course, my parents said that because they knew I would get a reasonable number of books. Then, they went to a movie theater and grocery shopping. It was my dream come true! So many books caught my eyes and they were all so interesting. I ended up spending about five hours there, and I had six new books in my bag on the way home. The list of books I got for my birthday are as follows:

*The Great Gatsby* / F. Scott Fitzgerald (English)
> I've already read this twice in Korean, but I wanted to read it
> in the original version.

*To Kill a Mockingbird* / Harper Lee (English)
> The title sounds interesting, doesn't it?

*East of Eden* / John Steinbeck (Korean)
> I am looking forward to reading this as I liked *The Grapes of
> Wrath* so much.

*Thus Spoke Zarathustra* / Friedrich W. Nietzsche (Korean!)
> I know it won't be easy, but I wanted to try this at least once!

*On Writing* / Stephen King (Korean)
> To improve my writing, hehe.

*America* / Jean Baudrillard (Korean)
> Hopefully it will help me understand the US better.

Other books I was interested in were *The Age of Innocence, 1984, Catch-22, Les Miserables* and *Gone with the Wind*. But I didn't want to buy too many books at once, so these will have to wait until I finish the other six first.

After the trip to the bookstore, mom made my favorite spicy chicken dish for our dinner. The food was awesome, and I couldn't be more relaxed, enjoying the evening with my family. There was nothing fancy, but to me it was definitely the best birthday.

## Summer Vacation

JULY 14TH 2009 — I love how Summer is full of energy. When Summer approaches, I start thinking about beaches, mountains, or some exotic places, wondering what this year's vacation will be like. With a breathtaking view of nature, dazzling sunshine and fresh breeze, I feel so alive. I sometimes wonder if my love for summer has something to do with my name. In my given name there are two characters: "Ha" means Summer and "jin" means star.

I came home late tonight from a three-day trip to Gangwon province, the north-east region of Korea. We were a group of six friends, three girls and three guys, all professional players. It may sound like three couples, but actually it's one couple and four close friends all together. I wish I were part of the couple, but I have yet to find the right man for me. Yet, I still have wonderful friends with whom I can take a vacation!

First day, we went directly to the small resort we booked. The cottage had two rooms with a kitchen and a living room, just as we hoped. Checking in was easy and quick, and we walked to the beach. It was windy and the beach was almost empty. We took off our shoes and felt the soft sand. We smelled the ocean, exchanged glances, and immediately ran into the sea. The water was pretty cold, but we all had fun laughing and chasing each other.

Coming back to our cottage, we had an outdoor barbecue. We grilled meat and fresh vegetables, and had nice Australian wine. It was so relaxing and no one needed to check the time! Over the dinner, we talked about baduk, future plans, shared memories, and so on.

Second day, we slept in and had a big brunch. Coffee, toast, scrambled eggs, sausages, and some fruit. The food was good, but the time we had was even better. When we were all fully awake and active, we left the cottage. Walking to the beach would have been nice, but unfortunately it was raining. So, we got in the car and drove off without a clear destination. The countryside was lovely, and we enjoyed the rainy view and conversations. Once in awhile the rain would pause, and we stopped our car to get some fresh air and stretch our legs. At one point we found an old local café, and had some hot drinks and snacks.

Do you wonder if pro players play baduk on their vacations? Some do and some don't. We didn't play any on this vacation, though. I would say in general pros prefer not playing because baduk is something they do almost every day anyway. Yet, I do know a few pros who just love to play baduk whenever they get the chance. For them, playing baduk is life itself.

Today was sunny and clear. We went biking along an idle railway in the morning and headed home after lunch. Time flew like an arrow. I felt a bit sad the vacation was over already. Now that I am living in Daejeon, it was even harder to say goodbye to my friends. Yet, now I have another special memory with them, and I am grateful for that.

# 2009 US Go Congress in DC

AUGUST 12TH 2009 — The Korea Baduk Association has a program that sends one or two professional players to major baduk events outside the three countries, Korea, China, and Japan. This year they had an announcement for a trip to the US Go Congress, and I received the ticket thanks to my English ability.

I was so excited about this opportunity because this was not only my first Go Congress, but also a baduk event that is designed to be fun. As a baduk prodigy, all baduk events I attended were for intense training or official tournaments. The US Go Congresses and the European Go Congresses are known in Korea as fun events, and I had hoped to be there someday.

The 2009 US Go Congress was held in George Mason University, located in Fairfax, Virginia. It takes an hour by subway or a 40 minutes' drive to go to downtown DC. The campus was huge and the buildings mostly looked similar. I stayed at the student dormitory named "Commonwealth", where two rooms shared one bathroom in between. In each room, there were two beds, two desks, and two chairs. When I travel as a pro player, I usually get to stay at hotels. So it was quite surprising to notice that there was no toilet paper, soap, or towels in the room. By the time I realized this, the only convenience store in the campus was already closed. So the very first night, I walked to the closest 7-Eleven, which was about two miles away.

Before coming to the Congress, I had seen some pictures, most of which were pro players lecturing in front of a group of people. Seeing those pictures, I imagined lecturing before serious looking players, who would nod and raise interesting questions. It would be difficult, but pretty cool at the same time. Yet as soon as I checked my schedule that night, my expectations broke into pieces because I was only doing simultaneous games. Later I learned that only the pros with long teaching careers were assigned to give lectures, unless otherwise requested by the pros.

## Daily Life

During the Congress, my life was relatively regular. A day started with 8 o'clock breakfast at the cafeteria in Southside. They had scrambled eggs, bacon, potatoes, bread, and fruit. The food was the same every morning, but the Congress was over by the time I felt like having something different.

First morning, I followed other people to the Johnson Center, where everyone was playing in the US Open. Yet, in the beginning there wasn't much for me to do, so I learned to relax in the morning. One thing I found interesting was that the time limit for the US Open was two hours each, longer than the average time limit for professional matches in Korea. For amateur tournaments, you often have somewhere between 10 minutes to 40 minutes each. I guess American players enjoy the process of thinking while Korean players like to play faster and more often.

After lunch I started my official activities. Simultaneous games twice a day at the student union building, and hanging out with other players. Also, I would review some games for the players who were brave enough to ask for it. Not many players did that though. Have you heard of the saying, "the brave gets the review"? Haha. Anyway, it would be around 9 p.m. when I finished all the day's activities, a bit tired but happy to be free. Then, I would go back to the main hall of Johnson Center, where most players came to hang out in the evening. We enjoyed beer and chips while playing baduk there until late at night.

## Pair Go

On Thursday, there was a Pair Go event. My partner was WJ, an AGA 5-dan from Seattle. At first we didn't expect to be one of the top pairs, assuming there would be many stronger teams. But our team was placed as the last pair in the first table, among professionals and high dans. My partner seemed quite stressed about the games, but he managed to play very well and we ended up winning both games. It was certainly nice to win, but more than that I had a lot of fun playing pair go. That night, we celebrated our success with some beer, even though we didn't know that we 'won' the Pair Go Championship. So, we were really surprised to be named as 'Pair Go Champion' at the closing ceremony, days after the Pair Go event. There, we received a cool trophy, a beautiful vase and $25 gift certificate each.

## Closing Banquet

The main hall looked totally different decorated for the banquet. Decent looking round tables, covered with burgundy tablecloths, were fully set with upscale dining utensils. Delightful live music was being played on the stage, and well-dressed people were talking to each other pleasantly. Just a day before, the same people were sitting at the same hall in congress t-shirts before nondescript Go tables. Just as I found my seat, the waiters started to serve salad with goat cheese as an appetizer. The salad was so fresh and tasty! The main dish was a combination of grilled salmon, chicken roll and orzo with a bit of green vegetables. They were all amazing, especially the salmon. Then we received desserts, wild berries and chocolate!

When I almost finished my dinner, someone went on the stage and said "I believe all of you had your dessert." That was the start of the closing ceremony. Allan [Abramson], the president of the AGA, gave us an address saying that this years' Go Congress, too, was successful and he was already looking forward to the next one. Then the awards ceremonies of various tournaments followed: 9x9, 13x13, Die Hard, Blitz, Pair Go, Ing masters and US Open etc. Last, they introduced the director of the next year's Congress, who announced briefly about the date and location. And she sang a beautiful song about next year's event.

Time passed so fast. As I was leaving the main hall after the closing banquet, I couldn't believe that the Congress was almost over already. It was becoming even nicer to be here by this point; I knew more people, calling their names and asking how they were doing. I could get to any building in the campus without getting lost. And I knew how to get to the convenience store, its opening hours, the phone number of the closest Domino's, and the fares of buses and subways to downtown DC.

I had so much fun during the Congress, though. I could see genuine enthusiasm for baduk. Sometimes they were as serious as professional players, but sometimes they would enjoy the game like kids. No matter how strong, or how old, everyone could hang out with others so naturally. I was happy to be a part of such a warm community and wish I can go to more Congresses to come!

# Immunity

AUGUST 28TH 2009 — I lost a match yesterday. It was the preliminary first round of a major tournament. Though I didn't expect to pass the preliminary anyway, losing the game was still painful. There is no one word that can describe my feelings exactly, but close ones would be bitter, frustrated, sad, painful, gloomy, or disappointed.

Last night, I had several shots of whisky and went to bed at around 3:30 a.m. Why aren't I immune to the pain of defeat yet? I must have lost more than 100 important games so far. According to the Internet, our body creates memory cells as an immune system and prepare us for a similar kind of infections. Yet, doesn't my body understand that I need these cells for losing a match?

When I was younger I often cried after losing games. More than sadness or anger, I just couldn't stand the fact that I lost. I stopped crying as I got older, except for a few cases when the defeat was too painful.

One example was the determining match of the pro qualification in 2003. I was 15 years old, and my opponent was 3 years older than me. At the time I was the top player in the insei league, and she was somewhere between the top 5 and 10. Plus, I had about 80% winning record against her. Because of this, my friends all thought I would win and congratulated me even before the game. I got black, and the game seemed to be going well. I was ahead by about 3-4 points by the endgame, and I would probably have won the game if it were a normal insei league. Yet, I froze at the idea of becoming a pro, and started playing slack moves. I was so afraid of losing the game by an unexpected disaster. There was no disaster until the end, when I lost the game by a half point. After this game I felt so sad that I cried for three nights and four days. Well, maybe less. Anyway, I had to wait for one year to play at the pro qualification again, and I didn't make the same mistake twice.

Another painful loss was in 2006. It was a women's team competition among Korea, Japan, and China, and each team had five players. At the time this was the only international tournament for female players and its prize money was much higher than any domestic tournaments for women. You can imagine how competitive it must have been to qualify for the Korean team. In year 2006, I qualified there for the first time, and my team flew to Beijing to play the first round. This competition has a a "win and continue" format, just like the

GGAuction Cup. In short, it means you have two players playing at a time. Then, only the winner continues, to play the next player from another team. Being the newest and youngest in the team, I was encouraged to be the first player, and my first opponent was a Chinese player. There were so many cameras and journalists to cover the very first match of the competition, and I lost by a half point there. I felt so sad about the game that the entire Beijing experience was somewhat gloomy.

Considering my experiences with these defeats, I should be fine with the game yesterday, right? But… Why doesn't it seem to be the case?

# LASEK

SEPTEMBER 18$^{TH}$ 2009 — I was planning to resume my math studies and squash lessons when I came back from the US. Not that I had made special plans, but they were both fun and I didn't have anything else going on. I guess "life is what happens while you're busy planning other things" as John Lennon sang.

I got LASEK surgery, rather spontaneously. When I came back home, my father told me about a promotional discount for the surgery. Although I knew that there were such surgeries, I used to think I was fine with my glasses. Yet, I met some people recently with positive feedback, and I became somewhat interested in the surgery. So, when my dad reminded me of the possibility, I decided to go for it. We made the reservation right away, and soon the day came.

"Just look at the green light. It is an easy surgery. Don't be nervous." The nurse seemed busy arranging the surgery room. She wasn't even looking at me while she was preparing me for the surgery.

"What happens if I move my pupils during the surgery?"

"You will be in big trouble. Don't do that."

"What happens if I close my eyes during the surgery?"

"You can't, even if you wanted. Don't worry."

"Anything else?"

"Nope. Oh, by the way, don't be surprised when the doctor pours cold water into your eyes."

"What? Cold water? In my eyes?"

As the nurse told me the surgery was easy and quick. All I had to do was to focus on the green light in front of me. During the process, the light would go from clear to vague, then clear again. It didn't hurt. I felt water pouring into my eyes, but it wasn't bad either.

The hard part came after the surgery, though: It was painful to keep my eyes open. When I tried, my eyes would feel stiff and tired. Any light was too bright for me. Plus I received three types of medicine to put into my eyes every hour and additional pills to take with water. They told me not to wash my face or hair for a week, not to wear make-up for four weeks, not to drink alcohol for four weeks and to wear sunglasses outside for three months. Not being able to see well, the most I could do was to listen to audio books, radio or TV. I couldn't even look at a computer monitor or cell phone screen. But now that several days have passed, things are much better. After all that, it's truly amazing that I can see things without my glasses!

By the way, I have another update. It seems like I will be taking another trip to the US in a few weeks. Kwon Kapyong 7p is the most famous baduk teacher in Korea. His baduk academy is the oldest, and he has produced over 35 professional players so far, including Lee Sedol 9p, Choi Chulhan 9p, Park Jeonghwan 9p, and many other top players. Among Mr. Kwon's students are not only professional players but also successful people in other areas. For example, one of his baduk students later went to a private boarding school in Connecticut called the Kent School, and is currently studying at Columbia University.

The father of this student believed that studying baduk contributed to his son's academic success, and donated some funds to

Kent School so that the school can introduce Go to other students. The school became convinced that Go could benefit Kent students. So, the Kent School invited Mr. Kwon, and he gladly accepted the invitation.

Mr. Kwon looked for an assistant to help with the teaching and translating since he didn't speak English, and offered me the task. Of course, I agreed to do it without any hesitation. I am going to Seoul in a few days to discuss this trip with Mr. Kwon. I am really excited about the project, and teaching baduk in this elite high school.

# Kent School

OCTOBER 20^TH 2009 — I had a good trip to the US and I am back in Daejeon now. Going to Kent School was definitely my longest travel time ever. First, I took a bus for two and a half hours to the airport, flew 14 hours to New York, and had a car ride for another two and a half hours to the Kent School in Connecticut. This doesn't include all the waiting, border control, baggage claim, and so on. Yes. It was exhausting, but worth it.

It was already after midnight when the driver stopped the car. Mr. and Ms. Cloutier, Mr. Kwon's hosts, warmly welcomed us. A fire was burning in the fireplace, and they invited us in for a glass of wine, some scrambled eggs and English muffins. I was touched by their hospitality then, and even more when I learned that Mr. and Ms. Cloutier usually go to bed before 10 p.m. We had a nice warm dinner there, and then I moved to the house of my host, Mr. Marais.

The following day was Saturday. I woke up around 7 a.m. and went out for a short walk since last night was too dark to see anything. The air was chilly and crispy. Just a few minutes walk outside the house, I couldn't believe what I was seeing. The autumn colors on the trees in the mountains, the shiny Hudson River and peaceful atmosphere were absolutely beautiful. I walked for a while along the river, thinking how lucky I was to be there.

In the afternoon, as the time of the first lecture approached I began to get nervous. It was my first time translating in front of so many people. In addition, I was intimidated by the fluent English of the Korean students who gave us a campus tour earlier that day. I even asked Mr. Kwon if he would rather have a Korean student translate in my place. He insisted I do it, though, because I understood what he had to say. The lecture began on time, and about 15 people were in attendance, including three teachers. Mr. Kwon explained the origins of baduk and the known benefits of the game, before explaining how to capture stones and how to win a game. It turned out translating for Mr. Kwon was not difficult, the hard part was answering questions. I was amazed how complex their questions were, and we had to teach them a lot more than we planned to be able to answer their questions.

Sunday morning, we had a small group session at Mr. Cloutier's house. The plan was to teach Mr. and Ms. Cloutier, their daughter Alexa, and her fiancée, Tim. Yet, only Mr. Cloutier was available, so he invited Dr. Nadire and his twins, Ryan and Liam. Dr. Nadire teaches mathematics in the Kent School, and he was interested in all games. I think one of his Ph.D.s was about Game Theory. His nickname was Doctor Doctor, because he had two Ph.D.s. Mr. Kwon and I briefly demonstrated the few rules of baduk, and we helped them play each other. It was interesting to see how fast they picked up things!

Following the session, we went to Kent's downtown for sightseeing. The downtown was pretty. There were fancy restaurants, cafés, book stores, a public library, a few art galleries, etc. According to Mr. Cloutier, Maine and Connecticut are renowned for their beautiful scenery of Hudson River, and the particular style of the artists who mainly painted it. Appreciating the fairy-tale-like view and peaceful atmosphere of Kent, I could see why there were many art galleries in such a small town.

Our second lecture at Dickinson Auditorium went more smoothly than the first one. We taught some basic techniques and asked for two volunteers to come forward. It was Mr. Kwon's idea that we have two people play each other on a demonstration board and we comment on their game as it goes. It was quite successful. Everyone seemed focused on following what was going on.

That night, Mr. and Ms. Cloutier invited us to an American barbeque party. They made a fire in the fireplace and prepared burgers, sausages, vegetables, and a bottle of red wine. The food was amazing, and we had such a nice time talking about Kent School and the professional player's life.

On Monday, I got up early and walked to the school. It was fresh autumn weather, sunny and windy. The campus was more lively and cheerful with students around. I stopped one of them and asked if he knew where the dean's office was. He didn't know, but told me that there was a meeting in a minute for all students. I asked "Can I see?" and he said "I think so. Just follow me, I am going there." At the meeting, they talked about H1N1 flu, a campaign for the homeless, a blood donation truck, group photos, etc.

As I was having lunch with Mr. Kwon at the Dining Hall, Mr. MacLeod greeted us and shook hands with us. He was a math teacher, the chess club advisor, and football coach at the same time. He said he was interested in learning Go, but couldn't come to the lecture because he would be out of town for the weekend. As we were talking with Mr. MacLeod, another teacher approached and greeted us. He was a French teacher, and knew about Go through the French novel titled *La Joueuse de Go* (or *The Girl Who Played Go* in English).

Our next lecture was in Mr. MacLeod's math class, where there were about a dozen students. We showed them part of the *Hikaru no Go* anime and taught them basic rules of the game. Because we had only a short time, we covered only a few things and let them play. Later, I asked Mr. MacLeod if he thought students liked it. He said "some of them seemed to enjoy it. But you know, they at least got to know what it is. That's what matters." I agreed.

That night, Mr. Kwon and I went to Mr. MacLeod's house, where the chess club met. He said usually six or seven students came to the chess club. This time, however, Mr. MacLeod advertised that Go masters would demonstrate the game, and pizza would be served for everyone. Thanks to Mr. MacLeod's PR, or perhaps thanks to the pizza, more than 20 students showed up. That night, 10 large pizzas and six baduk sets were not enough to accommodate everyone.

Next morning was cloudy and chilly. We had a relaxing time until lunch, where we had a meeting with the Kent Math Team members. Because there are many mathematicians among Western players, we thought the math team would be a good place to promote the game. Yet, the result was a bit disappointing. About a half of the members were Korean students, and they said they wanted to do something western while they studied in the US. I guess that's understandable.

As our last official activity, we were invited to have dinner at Dr. Nadire's house. The dinner was Moroccan style couscous with lamb and vegetables. It was my first time trying any food from Africa, and I loved it. Over the nice dinner, we talked about establishing a Go club at Kent. Nothing was certain then, but it seemed promising. We played baduk after dinner.

I suppose it will be tough to get a Go club going in the beginning since they don't have a strong player. Still, I hope they will manage and grow to be an active and strong club.

## Beginnings

OCTOBER 22ND 2009 — I received a nice email from the Kent School today!

*Dear Hajin.*

*I don't know why I suddenly feel very interested in Go, and now I regret that I missed the first three Go courses. I went on the internet to find some videos about the game, but I am a bit confused. I guess I will read the books you gave us to work on this fantastic game!*

*By the way, we also established a Go club in Kent! I think this game will be more and more popular in our school. — Joe*

I was so happy to hear that their Go Club got off the ground. It will be so nice to have Kent's bright students become a part of the next generation of the US Go community. Considering how rare it is for Americans to come across baduk in their life, I was lucky to be born in Korea, or more precisely, born as a daughter to my parents.

My father learned baduk when he was a freshman in his middle school. His school had the strongest baduk club in the country; one of his classmates even became a pro later on. Thanks to this environment, he had easy access to baduk books and materials, and he made fast progress throughout his three years at the school. When he entered high school, though, he realized he shouldn't divide his time between two areas. He was tempted to pursue a career as a professional player, mainly because he loved the game. Yet, he was too realistic to make such a liberal choice, and he stopped playing baduk in order to devote his time to his studies.

My father entered one of the top universities in Korea, majoring in electronic engineering and mathematics. He picked up baduk again as a hobby in college, and it's been his favorite game ever since. He also introduced the game to my mother so that they could play together. Today, my father gets four handicap stones from me, and my mother gets seven.

As I mentioned in an earlier entry, I was 5 years old when my parents sent me to a local baduk academy for the first time. My parents would play baduk on Sundays in our living room, and I observed them. At their baduk level, they could teach me themselves, but they thought I'd be better off learning from a proper teacher from the beginning. So, I started at this small baduk academy with other kids, and when I became good enough to have a game, my dad and mom played with me at home once in awhile.

This is how I started playing baduk, and I don't remember the time I didn't know about the game. Baduk was always at our home, and learning the game was so natural for me. I sometimes wonder how my life would have been different if my parents weren't players. Would I still have become a baduk professional? Well, I guess there is no point in wondering about what I will never know. What matters is that I did start baduk, lived it, and will probably be playing it for the rest of my life.

## TOEFL

November 1ST 2009 — Other than teaching baduk at an elite high school in the US, I've also been studying for the TOEFL for the last few months. If you are not familiar with it, the TOEFL is an English proficiency test. Earlier, I mentioned that I've been searching for a university to apply to. In fact, I found an international university in my hometown, Daejeon. Their program is 100% in English, and they have an admission policy that only looks at your TOEFL score and some essays. The only requirement is that your score must be higher than a 95 out of 120. To tell you the sad story, I took the test once already and received a 94. Luckily I had just enough time to take the test again before the application deadline, and I made my second attempt just yesterday.

Studying baduk and a foreign language have a few things in common. First, you can't rely on either studying or doing it for real by themselves. You have to do both. Some people hope to improve only by playing or speaking with friends, but eventually you need to study. But studying by itself won't work either. Second, there are fundamentals you must understand. People who have solid grammar can speak relatively good English in any context, and players who understand shapes and the flow of stones can navigate any stage of a game. Last, anxiety invites mistakes. Even a strong player makes simple mistakes when she is nervous. Likewise, even a good English speaker can make mistakes because of stress. For example, I can usually speak well, but I was so nervous at the speaking session of the TOEFL yesterday. Oh well.

Anyway, my score is supposed to come back in three weeks. Last time I took the test, I was checking the website for my score every half an hour for a week or so. It was so hard for me to wait for my score because for my whole life I didn't have to wait. You know, in baduk you win or lose. You don't wait for the result. So I registered for three weeks of driving lessons. I need to get a driver's license at some point, and it will be a good distraction from the upcoming score. Haha. Actually I doubt anything can distract me from the score, but it will still be better than nothing.

# The 5th Second Birthday

NOVEMBER 11TH 2009 — Have you heard of a second-birthday? Well, I made one up for myself because the day felt like a new birthday to me. I was walking through a long and dark hallway for years, until I finally reached this grand gate. As the door opened, glaring sunlight from the other world poured in. The day was November 11, 2004, exactly five years ago.

*"I resign. Congratulations."*

*She offered her hand over the board and shook mine lightly. I couldn't see her eyes nor say anything. I fixed my eyes on the board and remained silent. Soon enough, she stood up and left the room. My heart was beating so fast and loud that it felt as if it would explode any moment. I closed my eyes. I could not think of anything else, but repeating, "I made it. I am a pro now."*

The above paragraph is from my old diary, but I could easily write it again even without the diary if I wanted to. The scene is still vivid in my head. I doubt I will ever forget that day, that moment. I also remember how my parents were outside the playing room when I came out after the last game. You know, they were supposed to be working in Daejeon, two hours from Seoul. I asked them why they came, and they said, "It seemed important to see you regardless if you won or lost." Last year when I lost the last match by a half point, my parents weren't there. Though we never talked about it, I guess they regretted that they weren't there to console me.

Eleven years of playing, seven years of training at my teacher's house. All the thrills, excitement, difficulties, and pressures melted like snow in my mind. The further you walk this path, the harder it becomes to change direction. So, most people walk this path until either they become pro or are forced to give up because of their age or some external factor. If you become pro, your career as a baduk player is wide open. If you fail to become pro, however, your challenge becomes even tougher inside or outside the baduk community. That's why there are heavy pressures on every baduk prodigy's shoulders, and why passing a pro test is special.

The last five years have been mixed. My performance as a professional player has been decent, but it could have been better. There were challenges in life, while I had some of the most wonderful experiences. Overall, though, I am happy with my experiences as a professional player so far, and I think I am ready to move on to a new stage of my life.

## Professional Pride and Sponsorship

NOVEMBER 19TH 2009 — I attended the annual meeting of the Korean professional players' union today. I missed this meeting last year because I had to stay at YBA, but I was free now and curious to see the latest developments in the professional world.

The Korea Baduk Association (KBA) was founded in November, 1945 by the late Master Cho Namchul, who came back to Korea in 1943 after becoming professional 1-dan in Japan. Master Cho introduced modern baduk (at the time, Koreans were playing a traditional style called "Sunjang." In this system, the first 17 moves were fixed by a rule.), creating an organizational structure as a national governing body of baduk and a professional player system. After that, he led the development of baduk in Korea for decades, and now the KBA is a large organization with over 30 full-time employees. Master Cho is by far the person Korean players respect the most as the father of modern Korean baduk.

When Master Cho established the KBA, his primary objective was to organize professional tournaments like the ones in Japan. Later on, he let other people work on the administration and management of the KBA, while he became an active player in tournaments, but important decisions were still made in consultation with him and other senior professional players. Over time, respecting and consulting professional players became part of the organizational culture of the KBA. Now we have the professional players' union, in which all professional players in Korea are automatically registered, and the union's influence on the management of the KBA is powerful.

Since the beginning of the KBA, professional players were paid for playing matches starting from the preliminary rounds, regardless of your result. This model was from Japan, and the KBA adopted many policies from them. In order to maintain this structure, the KBA has limited the number of new professional players each year, and it was generally understood by sponsors and fans that professional players should always be paid whenever they play.

Times have changed and circumstances are different now, however. The hot topic of the meeting today was whether we should allow sponsors to offer tournaments that pay prize money only for a certain number of top places. This is an economically difficult time, and we are grateful to our sponsors. We should do as much as we can to maintain them, but where is the line?

The KBA has policies regarding professional event sponsorship. I don't know much about them, but one thing I do know is that a sponsor has to put in a lot more money than what the public sees. Paying for the preliminary round was never a deal breaker when the number of pro players was relatively small. The number has increased grad-ually, though, and today we have over 200 pros in Korea. Though each player's per-match stipend is not very big, all together support-ing the preliminary round starts to seem like an unnecessary burden for prospective sponsors. So, one potential sponsor proposed that they will offer higher prize money for the main round in return for not paying for the preliminary. This is probably more attractive to the sponsors as better public exposure. But, if we allow them, what about the other sponsors?

In the current system, even if you are not in the top 50 or so, you can still make decent money by playing matches. There are about 10-20 tournaments per year, and all of them pay for the preliminary rounds. My last year's income from tournaments was about $40,000 USD. By the way, this reminds me of one conversation I had in the Kent School. I was talking with a French teacher who knew a little about baduk. I said, "I am a professional Go player." Then he said, "In America, that means you get paid when you play." So I said, "Yes, that's what I meant." He didn't seem to believe me though.

Professional players fear that once we allow a tournament that does not pay for the preliminary round, sooner or later all sponsors will ask for the same deal. If this happens, the strongest players will have higher incomes while the majority of the pros will have much less. It also hurts most professional players' pride that they will have to play without payment. And yet, if it comes to whether we want to have a tournament or no tournament, of course any tournament would be better than nothing.

In today's meeting, the union agreed to draw a line like, "Only tournaments with more than one million dollars of total budget can have a preliminary round without payment." The amount in that sentence is not exact, but it's close enough. In my opinion, though I like the current system as a pro player myself, this change is more fitting to the world in which we are living today. I believe not all professional players should make their living by tournaments alone.

Rather than protecting the old system, we should develop more career options for pro players.

# Life and Death Problems

NOVEMBER 26<sup>TH</sup> 2009 — Last night, I was half-lying on my bed,
staring at the baduk board on the wall. My room has a magnetic
board on the wall, because I thought I might practice lecturing baduk
in English. So far, I haven't used the board for much, but I would
make a few life and death problems on the board and stare at them
whenever I have some down time. It also feels somewhat comforting
to have the big baduk board in the room. Baduk has sometimes been
something I wanted to escape, but at the same time it's my closest
companion. Mom saw me staring at the wall (from her angle she
couldn't see the board) and asked me what I was doing. I told her I
was solving life and death problems (L&D for short).

L&D has been my favorite area of baduk from the very beginning. If there was a career in solving L&Ds instead of playing entire
games, I would definitely have chosen that. As a child, I liked to play
with puzzles or similar sorts of toys. Then once I got into baduk,
nothing was more interesting than L&D problems. I would over-do
my L&D homework, while neglecting opening or joseki books. Consequently, I was good at reading and local battles, but my weakness
was global perspectives and long-term plans.

As I was getting close to the pro level, my teacher came up with
this special L&D training method. He assigned each of us a L&D
book, and gave us one week. In the book, there were about 200 problems without answers, and we were to solve all of them and memorize
the answers, without writing the answers on the book. The book had
to be kept clean. At the end of the week, we went to the teacher with
the book, and we had to present our answers to the teacher one by
one, from the first problem to the last. Then, the teacher would either say, "next," or put a stone on the board (meaning, the answer

was incorrect). By the time I got through the entire book, I would have about 25 baduk stones on the board. The sight of the stone pile saddened me, because I had to hold a 2-inch baduk board above my head for one minute per wrong problem. You can imagine how serious this training was. At that time, I wasn't sure if L&D was fun anymore.

When I became a professional player, no one forced me to do such training, and I recovered my joy in solving L&D. The new trouble, though, was that it's rare to find L&D problems that are difficult enough for my level. Once in a while new problems would circulate among young pros, and I would happily work on them whenever I had them, like today. The problems I was solving last night were from my pro friend, who got them from a Japanese pro.

One funny incident from the Kent School: Mr. Kwon and I were having dinner with a few teachers who took interest in baduk. One of them asked what he was supposed to "think" in order to find "better moves." There could be many answers to that question, but they were all beginners who just learned liberties and atari. So I said, "Think about math. You just learned how to solve 1+1, but playing a game is like solving calculus. In math, you work on lots of exercise problems as you move up to a higher level. It's the same in Go, and you can exercise by solving Life and Death problems."

I thought my answer was clear, but they all looked shocked or puzzled. Then I realized that they were frightened by the word, "life and death". Life and Death problems! How come I never noticed it may sound severe? Haha.

One quick update! I got 100 on the TOEFL, a higher score than the university's admission requirement. The next step is to write admission essays, submit my application, and see if I can get an interview with them.

# Baduk Studies

December 1ˢᵀ 2009 — In Korea, students can choose baduk as a major. Though it's only available at one university for the moment, maybe there will be more schools in the future offering the major. In Myongji University, there is a department of Baduk Studies, and they accept 30 new students each year. What do you think Baduk Studies is about?

One of my dad's acquaintances attended the International Conference on Baduk, and asked my dad if I would be interested in seeing the materials. I gladly agreed, and the materials arrived today. I heard a few things about majoring in baduk, but I actually didn't know much about what one studied there. Having read these materials, however, I think I have a better sense of the program and the field.

In the conference handbook, there were research papers about various subjects such as "Elo-type Rating Systems for Professional Players", "Confucius and Baduk", "Baduk in Vietnam", "Effective Baduk Exhibitions", "Baduk Education", and so on. It was my first time to actually read something from "Baduk Studies", and they were more interesting than I expected. My favorite paper was the one about Confucius. The thesis argued that the old interpretation that Confucius didn't regard baduk highly was actually a misunderstanding. The author suggested that more evidence illustrated that Confucius knew how to play the game and appreciated it. Along the way of building his argument, the author cited many quotes and records of Confucius, and they were quite intriguing. Plus, I believe this research is not only interesting but contributes to the promotion of baduk in many ways.

I considered majoring in Baduk Studies earlier this year, but decided not to. I had a few reasons, the main one being my curiosity to study something else in a university. Though studying baduk and baduk studies are quite different, I didn't like the idea of limiting my world to baduk. My candidates were English Literature, Philosophy, Psychology, or Economics, but now I am very much hoping to study Business Administration at SolBridge. The more I learn about the school and its program, the more I like it. Fingers crossed for my application!

# New Year, New Start, New Direction

JANUARY 3$^{RD}$ 2010 — Another new year has just begun. Every year about this time, I feel hopes and fantasies float in the air. Where will my life boat go? Will I have a fresh wind to help me where I plan to go, or will I run into some wild storm that throws me somewhere unexpected? Storms would be tough, but I am not afraid of them. Often these storms make my journey thrilling and interesting. After all, it's the difficulties and challenges that make me stronger, right? I like the quote from *Twilight* that says, "Without the dark, we would never see the stars."

Last year's highlight was that I played the best-of-three final round against Rui Naiwei 9p, and I visited the US Go Congress and the Kent School. Then, I got LASEK surgery, a driver's license, and read a total of 33 books. Among them, my favorite was definitely *Anna Karenina*. What a masterpiece!

A few days ago, I made a big decision for the new year. The Korea Baduk Association (KBA) is setting up a special training team for 2010 Asian Games in Guangzhou. There will be three gold medals for baduk in the Asian Games, and the KBA is taking the event very seriously. This national training team is invitational, and I got a phone call from the women's team coach about a week ago that he would like to have me on the team. The Asian Games will be in November, so it'd be a year-long commitment. I would need to move back to Seoul, and stop most of my non-baduk activities. I was tempted to do so. Even my parents encouraged me to join the team. After a few days of debating, I decided it was time to move on. I don't know if I will get accepted at SolBridge, but I have a good feeling about it. My admission interview is in two days, so I will do my best to get in.

If I become a college student, I want to devote myself to the school life, with not as much baduk. So far, my schools were always for baduk, and I only dreamed about having a typical student life. University is not the same as high school or middle school, but I will still be happy to experience some form of a students' life. Anyway, I am so excited about the new start! Happy new year!

# Part III

# *University*

## Admission Interview

January 5<sup>TH</sup> 2010 — Today, I had my university admission interview at Solbridge International School of Business. The school is relatively new and I haven't known of their program for long, but it became my dream school from the moment I first visited their website. The website was modern and professional. Pictures showed many international faculty members and students, and the curriculum seemed interesting. In addition, the school was in my hometown, Daejeon, and I could easily commute to school from home.

Dad gave me a ride this morning. The school doesn't have a big campus, just a tall and modern building. It's located in the east part of Daejeon, close to the Daejeon train station. In fact, my discovery of this school was thanks to its location. One day I was going to the train station to go to Seoul, and saw this nice building on the way. I wondered what the building was for, so I searched online. That's how I found the school's website.

I walked into the school lobby with my dad and fell in love from the first sight. My dad was very impressed, too. It was modern and stylish with a somewhat international atmosphere. I told my dad that he didn't need to wait for me, and went to the waiting room for the applicants, on the 10<sup>th</sup> floor. Several students were sitting in the room, and there were some drinks and snacks prepared. Later, two student assistants came in with paper bags of sandwiches and soft drinks for everyone and announced the interview order.

The interview was conducted in a business style meeting room. There were three professors in the panel, one American and two Korean. We only spoke English throughout the interview though. I expected them to ask me what baduk was, but to my surprise they all knew about the game already! One Korean professor even told me that he saw my game against Cho Hyeyeon on Baduk TV. I was happy that baduk was recognized by the professors, but it was a pity that I didn't get to say what I had written and memorized for this question.

I think the critical moment was when the American professor asked me, "Don't you want to advance your career as a professional player? Why do you want to come to our school?" No professional player could deny the dream to be a top player. I knew this question had to come up, but I froze when it actually did. So, I took a deep breath and said, "Competing at the top level is an attractive role for professional players, but I believe there are many other roles that players can take. My plan is to study international business here, and work for the global baduk community. We have many excellent professional players in Korea, but very few doing international work. I think I can do a lot more in this field." One of them asked, "Do you mean you want to work for the Korea Baduk Association?" So I said, "Yes, or even better for the International Go Federation." The professors were nodding as I was answering their questions, and I knew it was going better than I hoped.

The result will be announced on January 22$^{nd}$. Fingers crossed!

# Admission Essay #1
# The Winter Vacation

I have written three essays for my application to SolBridge. One about the winter I decided to move to my teacher's house when I was 9 years old, one about my trip to Europe in 2006, and the last one about my future plans. They were all very meaningful topics for me and I enjoyed writing and revising them. In the following three entries, you can find my essays in order.

— Ben Stein, speechwriter for American presidents Richard Nixon and Gerald Ford, once said; "the first step to getting the things you want out of life is this: Decide what you want." Although it sounds easy, not many people seem to be able to decide what they want. Some find their passion too late to develop it, and others do not realize what they really want to do. Despite the fact, however, I was fortunate that I got a chance to recognize early what I want.

A few days before my third winter vacation began, my father told me to come and sit beside him. He was drinking coffee with my mother on the couch in the living room. They looked unusually serious. So instead of asking what was going on, I sat beside them quietly. After a few seconds of silence, he asked me if I wanted to learn baduk professionally during the winter vacation. I was attending a private baduk institution five days a week at the time. Then he added, to do this, I would have to leave home for about 40 days.

I was frightened. Although I liked playing Baduk, I did not think that I could leave my family to do so for such a long time. Yet, on the other hand, the expectation of the new experience thrilled me. It sounded like an adventure of a fairy tale. Besides, it was obvious that none of my friends would undergo such training. I instinctively wanted to surprise my friends by telling them about my unique vacation. Looking back, I think I said 'yes' to my parents, because I wanted to seem brave.

The baduk academy was located in Ilsan, Kyungki-do, around three hours away from home by car. The teacher was a professional baduk player himself, and offered rooms in his house to the students who lived far away like me. My roommate was Yoo-Jin, the teacher's daughter. She was a year younger than me, and also studying baduk. Getting ready for the training, I vaguely expected it to be about five hours a day. In third grade, I had taken five classes every Thursday in school, and I always regarded it as a long journey, since every other day I studied less. That drove me to conclude that five hours would be long enough. But, I was wrong. From the very next day of my arrival, Yoo-Jin and I walked to the baduk academy by 9 o'clock every morning, and got out at 9 o'clock in the evening. Even after subtracting a 10-minute break that was occasionally given and 45-minute meal times for lunch and dinner, there were still about nine hours left for study.

It was an endless repetition of many types of baduk training. I played baduk against peers, received comments on those games from the teacher, studied professional players' game records, solved exercise problems and played baduk again. Moreover, I had to memorize well-known games of prestigious players as homework! While I was suffering the tediously long study schedule, all I could do to entertain myself was to chat with Yoo-Jin when the teacher was absent or to go out for ice cream during breaks.

By two weeks, I nevertheless began to be absorbed by the study. It was not merely because I got used to the living pattern, but I found myself improving in baduk. Deeper understanding of baduk and fewer mistakes clearly demonstrated that it was not an imaginary feeling but a visible development. The achievement brought me self-confidence and renewed passion for the game. Consequently, my winning percentage went up significantly and it led me to play more seriously. Since then, studying baduk no longer distressed me, but offered as much pleasure as hanging out with friends.

On the day my parents came to take me home, my head was full of complicated feelings. I missed home. Playing with my sister, watching TV cartoons and walking to the nearby park with my family had constituted my everyday life. Being away from home for a long time taught me how much I liked those moments. Yet, the new experience also showed me that there was a totally different life. I got close to Yoo-Jin, other peers and the teacher as well. Above all, I liked studying baduk there. Just as I was about to leave, I fortunately realized that what I wanted the most was to stay where I was and keep studying baduk. Ironically, wanting to seem brave led me to come there, and wanting to stay there made me brave. And, this time, it was my turn to ask the parents, "Could you let me stay here? I want to keep studying baduk. I think I am ready to leave home for that."

My parents seemed astonished, but respected my decision in the end. Even though I was determined and passionate, it was not always fun to study baduk. There were frustrations and despair from many defeats and slumps which I had to overcome. In addition, I had to sacrifice school tasks, friends' birthday parties and other fun activities. Yet, whenever it felt tough, I reminded myself that it was not anyone else, but I, who decided to pursue this venture. As a result, my long perseverance was rewarded. In November, 2004 – about seven years later – I received my professional certification in the game of baduk.

# Admission Essay #2
# My First Trip to Europe

*The Frog in The Well* is a well known fable from ancient China. The frog thinks his well is the best place in the world. One day, he brags of living in such a nice well to a turtle, who came from the Eastern Ocean, and recommends that he move into the well. The turtle, however, refuses the frog's offer, describing how big and great the Eastern Ocean is. Needless to say, the frog would not have been embarrassed if he had ever been to the Eastern Ocean at least once. The frog in this fable illustrates people, who consider their society as the greatest without ever being outside of it. I must confess that I, too, was one of them until a golden opportunity knocked on my life. In this essay, I will describe my first trip to Europe, and outline what I learned from it.

"Can you go to Europe instead of me?" Although Mi-Kyoung might have asked me not expecting to be accepted, the question immediately hit my heart. I always had a fantasy of Western countries. Mi-Kyoung was supposed to go to Europe with one professor and another professional Go player to participate in the Korean Ambassador's Cup Go Championships in Germany, France and the Netherlands. Yet, she had to cancel at the last minute, and thus was looking for someone to take her place. I met her by chance that day, and she noticed I could satisfy the only required condition: the candidate must be a professional Go player.

I quickly thought about the possibility. It was certain that the trip would not cost as much as usual, because the Korea Baduk Association promised to provide airfare, and the Go associations of each nation guaranteed overnight accommodations, meals and reasonable payment. So, the only problem was school. Because I was a junior in high school, three weeks' travel during the semester seemed impossible. However, a miracle has happened. My teachers discussed the matter and concluded that the trip would be much worthier for me than studying in school. Therefore, with Mi-Kyoung's recommendation and the school's approval, I was able to get on a plane to Berlin, Germany on the 24th of March, 2006.

Our team was composed of three people. Professor Hahn, who proposed and managed the Korean Ambassador's Cup, led the team. Hae-Won, a professional Go player and a popular commentator on Baduk TV took part as a 'beautiful professional player' from Korea. I was the youngest of the team and played the role of 'the most promising player'. We stayed in Europe for 20 days and visited Germany,

Austria, France, the UK, Belgium and the Netherlands. During the journey, we mainly participated in the Korean Ambassador's Cup as special guests from Korea, played teaching games with the participants, and lectured on the game of Go. Also, we had meetings with Korean ambassadors and diplomats, regional Korean Go communities, local Go players and board members of Go associations and clubs. Despite a full schedule, however, we were able to go sightseeing during the day because, thankfully, most of our appointments were either during lunch time or business hours.

There is a proverb that says "Better to see once than to hear a hundred times." Indeed, seeing and being in real Europe was far better than merely seeing it on TV and reading about it in books. Being exposed to totally different culture - language, architecture, food, climate, people's manners and lifestyle – strongly shocked me. First of all, I could not help but notice the importance of English. Whomever I met, no matter what their first language was, everyone tried to talk to me in English. At the time, I could barely greet people in English. Thus, even though I had so many things to ask and talk about, all I could do was just smile and nod or rely on Professor Hahn, who occasionally translated for me. I was embarrassed, and I firmly decided to study English. As a result, after a few years of effort, I do speak English now. Secondly, I noticed sophisticated citizenship. For example, drivers seemed to always yield to passengers and bikes. Also, most public transportation was handicap-friendly, and no one looked upset when an elderly woman on a wheelchair delayed the whole bus. Last, I was absolutely attracted by the beauty of various European cities and their romantic atmosphere. Graceful architecture from antiquity was so well-preserved that it felt as if Queen Marie Antoinette, William Shakespeare or Mozart would walk out and talk to me any time. Among all the charming cities, however, my favorite was Oxford in the UK. Exquisite buildings, fresh green quadrangles, small cafés and old bookstores were in great harmony. Ever since I have seen it, one of my secret dreams was to study in Oxford at least one day.

However, in terms of the game of Go, Korea was certainly an advanced nation. I met a great number of European Go players who wanted to come to Korea to experience the so-called 'heaven of Go players'. They were curious to see 24/7 Go broadcasting channels, the department of Baduk Studies in Myongji University and the Korea Baduk Association as well. In Europe, teachers, books and materials about Go were extremely inadequate. Amid these poor conditions, however, more people were enjoying the game of Go than ever before, and many of them were rather passionate about it. I assume it was because Go has something that attracts people. Although Go was not yet widely known in Europe, I found its future shining when bright professors and students of Oxford kept asking me about Go. Moreover, I realized that professional Go players should exist not only for competitions but also for the promotion of the game of Go and the development of Go players all over the world.

# Admission Essay #3
# My Future Plans

Why do people plan? Most people plan for tomorrow, next month, and next year so on. There is a saying that 'Life is what happens while you are busy planning other things.' Dwight D. Eisenhower, a former US president and Army general, said "In preparing for battle I have always found that plans are useless, but planning is indispensable." If life does not go as we planned and plans seem useless in battle, why is planning still important? The author of *The Little Prince,* Saint-Exupery, suggests the answer. He said, "A goal without a plan is just a wish." I think planning is like drawing a map that guides us to the destination we seek. Once we have a map, it will be easier and more efficient to find the way we should take. Also, the map would lessen the risk of getting lost in our long journey of life. In this essay, I describe how I constructed my map.

There are countless jobs and professions in this world. Among those, how am I going to choose the right one? How can I know what the best one, that fits my talents, characters and nature, is? The answer is in the very question. In order to find the best profession for me, I should know myself – my talents, character and nature – first.

I am a professional Go player. I have spent almost half my life to achieve this. Within the game of Go I can be competent, competitive and distinguishable. Another weapon I have is the language of English. Although many Koreans nowadays are fluent in English, the fact that very few professional Go players speak English makes me stand out from others. In addition, I always liked reading and writing; since I was young, I have been reading books and writing journals, short stories and essays. For example, I have read more than 20 books this year including *Anna Karenina* by Tolstoy and *East of Eden* by Steinbeck, and posted a few stories and essays under an anonymous pen name on Cyberoro, the internet Go site. Also I am good at traveling and meeting people. Thanks to my childhood that separated me from the family, I naturally developed adaptability and social skills. Though I did not recognize these abilities at first, as I traveled several times, I found myself to get along well with anyone, appreciate food of diverse ethnicities, and even enjoy having conversations with strangers.

There seems to be two ways to maximize my strength as a professional Go player. One is to become one of the top Go players in the world. Becoming the strongest player is an attractive option, but I have learned that sheer dedication and effort are not sufficient in achieving that goal. The other option is to become a leader in the global Go community. Working for an international Go association will provide me with opportunities to use my strength in Go. Maybe more importantly, however, I would be able to utilize my social and communication skills. I also expect that my competency in English will be an indispensable skill in communicating with the global Go community. Thus, I have chosen the second option.

The destination is set. And the next step is to draw the map. I began with a couple of important questions. What abilities are required in order to become the leader of international Go organization? And, how should I acquire these abilities? The answers to these two questions will be the navigator of my successful career. For the first question, I believe that profound understanding of both the game of Go and international organizations is critical. Also, an ability to collaborate with both national and regional sections of Go associations would be essential. Understanding of human resource management and cross-cultural management are probably important too. Then I concluded – for the second question – that the only ability that I possess now is the understanding of the game of Go. Fortunately, according to my research, the curriculum for the International Business major in Solbridge includes studies that will help me acquire aforementioned skills. Therefore, I decided to major in International Business.

As a college student, learning and studying will be my top priority. However, because my long-term goal is directly related to Go, I think constant activities in the Go world are important. Therefore, I will also keep playing professional Go matches and participate in many types of Go events all over the world. Moreover, I would like to establish a Go circle in the university and teach the game of Go to my schoolmates. Through teaching friends from various countries, I will see how different cultures affect people's way of thinking in the game of Go. And this observation would ultimately help me to prepare for the future career. After graduating, I want to continue with a Master's program for the deeper understanding. Then I will probably work in other fields for some periods of time to build diverse working experiences. As Louis Pasteur, a French scientist, famously said, "Chance favors only the prepared mind." I believe that only the prepared gets the right chance and translates it to success. Although the destination is far away and there probably will be lots of obstacles, I will follow my map and keep inching toward my destination.

# Calculus

JANUARY 23ʳᴰ 2010 — I checked the school's website every five minutes yesterday, and at some point it was there. I got in! With 100% tuition scholarship! I can't overstate how thrilled I was. This means I will be a college student starting in March. My life is going to change so much. Right after seeing the result, I sent messages to my friends with excitement. At least for that moment, I was the happiest girl in the world.

This morning, however, I had a chilling moment. I got up early, had a nice breakfast, and noticed that I had received an email from SolBridge. It was one of the Korean professors from the interview panel.

*Dear Ms. Hajin Lee,*

*Congratulations! You have received a very high score on your interview, and we are pleased and excited to have you in our program.*

*As a friendly warning, I would advise you to study at least basic calculus before the semester starts. I have seen a number of students having trouble with our mandatory mathematics classes for freshmen. Although we also offer a pre-calculus class for those students, I am afraid it might not be sufficient.*

To tell you the truth, I didn't even know what calculus was. I mean, I'd heard the word somewhere, but I'd never had to deal with it. So I asked my dad.

"Dad, is calculus difficult?"

"I would say so. Why do you ask?"

"I need to learn it before the semester starts."

"No way. What for?"

"SolBridge has a mandatory mathematics class for freshmen."

"Oh… do you want to look at some examples of calculus?"

He showed me some, and my first impression was, "what is this alien language?!"

It felt as if my beautiful sky was being covered by dark clouds that came from nowhere. I am not comfortable with math. It's a little better now because I had studied math for a few months last year, but I was still far from calculus. On the bright side, however, my dad and sister told me they will help, and I have over a month to prepare. I didn't have anything big planned for this time, so I guess I will devote my time to math.

## Empathy

FEBRUARY 19TH 2010 — I am studying math about 10 hours a day these days. As soon as I decided to study calculus, I bought two books. One came with online video lectures as a package, and the other one was just very thick, full of various math concepts and problems. Watching the online lectures is helping, but I still struggle to solve actual problems. When my sister explains, they look so obvious. But, whenever I try alone, many formulae get mixed up in my head and I am confused which one is which. Besides, every problem looks both similar and different at the same time! Is that even possible? These problems don't seem to confuse my sister or dad, though. Thinking about this, I realized that these complaints were eerily similar to the ones my baduk students had. Our conversations would go like this:

"Hey, did you already forget what I said last time? This is a bad shape, you obviously should have played here."

"Did you mention this before? I don't remember."

"Come on. Just add some stones here, and see it from this side."

"Ah! Isn't this a little different though?"

"Not in a meaningful way. Don't miss this next time, promise?"

"I will try."

Starting this year I've been teaching baduk to a group of children as a part time job. I thought the kids had forgotten what I taught because they weren't focused. Everything was so clear and easy in my mind. Yet, I am definitely not struggling with math because I'm not focusing, it's just confusing. I am thinking maybe this experience will make me more empathetic towards my students.

# A Miniature of Life

MARCH 2^ND 2010 — As my first semester started, I received sad news. Mr. Kim, one of my teachers from my baduk academy, had passed away. He had had liver cancer for about two months, and I visited him twice during that time. I wish I had visited him more often, but there is nothing I can do now.

Mr. Kim was amateur 6-dan, and taught students from beginners to low-dan at Mr. Cha's baduk academy. He was never my teacher directly, because I was already too strong for his classes when I went there, but he was always there. He would have lunch and dinner with us and sometimes give us advice on baduk or on life. Because our academy was relatively small, all students and teachers were just like a big family.

When Mr. Kim discovered his liver cancer, the doctor said it was already too late. I couldn't believe he got cancer. He seemed well and fit, and I didn't even notice that he was getting older. I thought he would be there forever. Yet he's gone now. It happened all so suddenly. What made me sadder was what I heard at the funeral: One of my old friends from the baduk academy told me that Mr. Kim was so proud of me when he heard that I got into an international university. When I told him that I was going to be a freshman soon, he replied, "You could've been the top player." So I thought he didn't like the fact that I had chosen to go to a university. He was like this, though. He wouldn't say nice things to me when I was around, but many people would tell me later how he was always proud of me.

Baduk is often called a miniature of life. It may sound philosophical or abstract, but I think it describes the game's characteristics well.

Baduk is not just about capturing or building territories. There are also plans, objectives, positional judgment, psychological strategies and so on. I am sure that if you observe the game with your philosophical eyes, you will find your own reasons why the game is considered to resemble life.

My own version is like this: Everyone starts with an empty board. In the early stage, players lay the groundwork for the game. A well-constructed opening leads to a better position, but it doesn't guarantee a victory. Wu Qingyuan (also known as Go Seigen), the living legend of the field, famously said "Baduk is harmony." Many players have different styles, but I believe the best strategy in the opening is to balance between territories and thickness, just like children should be educated both physically and mentally.

The busiest part of one's life may be one's 20s and 30s since a lot of events happen during these years. This is also true for baduk. Between the opening and endgame is the most complicated but also the most exciting part of a game. Attacks, invasions, reductions, and solidifying territories all happen around this time, and these actions often decide the winner and the loser. Finally, during the endgame, we settle and arrange what we have achieved.

Life and baduk are not the same, though. First, in life we don't start as equals. Second, there is no winner or loser. Third, in baduk we can always begin a new game. And this third difference is making me quite sad today.

## Logical or Emotional

MARCH 5$^{TH}$ 2010 — My first week at the university was just wonderful. I am so excited about my classes, new books, new classmates, and everything! Most of my classes are required ones, like Mathematics for Business, Computer Applications for Business, Critical Thinking, and Microeconomics. Yet, I am also taking some electives and noncredit classes such as Chinese I, English Comprehension, and English

Conversation. English Conversation is a non-credit class that meets every Friday evening. I knew the class time would be in conflict with some parties, but I'm not much interested in parties anyway.

When I entered the classroom with another Korean student five minutes before class began, the teacher of English Conversation, Mr. Philip Booth, was already writing something on the whiteboard. Philip was black, maybe in his late 20s or early 30s. He was wearing formal attire, looking serious.

Class began, and Philip introduced himself and made each of us do the same. There were six students in the classroom, including myself. When it was my turn to introduce myself, I didn't mention anything about baduk. I didn't mean to hide it, but I wanted to be a nondescript student rather than someone special. From elementary school to high school, I was always the special kid who played baduk, and I wished I could be more normal. So, I plan to keep my background to myself here at SolBridge, at least for the time being.

Today's topic was logic and emotion in conversations. According to Philip, we can divide every spoken conversation into two categories: logical and emotional. Logic contains evidence, facts and reasons, etc, and emotion is anything related to feelings. He said men tend to speak logically while women often speak emotionally. Then, he suggested that although emotional speech has many good aspects, we should know how to deal with logical conversations because 90% of business speech is logical. I asked him if we there was anything in between, and he said the two could be mixed, but always one prevails over the other.

Coming back home, I thought about what we discussed in the class. This is my study habit from baduk. You play a game and then review it later. Also, when I studied English in the study group, I wrote a one- or two-page summary of what we covered after each meeting. Now here I am studying in an international university, so it must have worked.

Philip's point about logic and emotion seems to work with baduk as well. I mean, there can be logical or emotional moves. For instance, when I ask you *'Why did you play there?'* If you answer *'I thought I would win this capturing race.'* That is a logical move. On the other hand, if you say *'It didn't feel right to let black take this whole territory.'* This would be an emotional move.

Just like in conversations, there are certain merits to emotional moves. No one can read perfectly, and sometimes your emotions or instincts will lead you to better results. Also, we should always remember that psychology is a big part of this game. For example, if you feel that your opponent is being safe, you should push harder than what you would usually do logically, because there is a good chance that your opponent will step back. Nevertheless, I would say about 90% of professional players' moves are logical. So, if you want to be stronger, learn how to deal with logical moves. Who knows, practicing how to speak more logically might help me play more logical moves in baduk, too!

# Balance

APRIL 17TH 2010 — It's Saturday after mid-terms week. I got up at 6:30 a.m. to take an early train to Seoul. I thought all my classmates must be asleep at this hour, and I hoped I could stay in bed as well. Yet, it was the first day of the preliminary round of the LG Cup International Baduk Championship. Though I really needed a relaxing weekend after my first serious exams, I was grateful that I could play this match without compromising my studies.

The KBA building was so crowded, with not only Korean players but also professional players from China, Japan, and Chinese Taipei. The LG Cup is one of a few tournaments that open their preliminary rounds to any professional player regardless of their nationality. Although I couldn't recognize most of the foreign pros' names except for several famous players, they all certainly had the atmosphere of professional players with serious expressions on their faces.

Happily greeting my fellow players, I sat at the seat indicated by my name plate. The board in front of me was empty and clean. Next to the board, a silver digital clock was displaying three hours plus 60 seconds 5 times overtime for each player. Staring at the empty wooden board, I suddenly felt like the board was looking at me, asking "where have you been?" I didn't know what to say.

It has been one and a half months since I became a college student. Compared to my 5-year professional baduk career, half a semester is only a short time. Nevertheless, I already feel more comfortable at school than I did at the tournament venues. For the first time in my life, I am fully attending a school without making excuses. On the other hand, I missed three tournaments in March, and two more in April because I didn't want to miss my classes. It was a dramatic change for me to choose something else over my matches, but I decided baduk is not my top priority anymore.

I am not sure where baduk should belong in my life. Balance and harmony are the most important concepts in baduk, and I have been training myself to consider it at all times. Maybe it's time for me to put this practice of balance into real life. Just as I keep a balance between territory and potential on baduk board, I will need to keep a balance between my baduk and everything else. I think I am leaving the tournament scene with my university life, but in my mind I am still a professional player. My understanding of being a professional player, though, will need to change. I lost my match today, but I wasn't as sad as I used to be. I guess it's time for me to find my new balance.

# Korean Ambassador's Cup in Prague

MAY 5ᵀᴴ 2010 — One fine day in April, I received a phone call from Mr. Jo, a manager at the KBA. He told me the KBA was looking for

a professional player to attend the 39th Korean Ambassador's Cup
International Go Tournament. At first I was going to refuse politely
because it was the middle of the semester. Midterm exams were over,
but classes were still going on as usual. Then, Mr. Jo said, "Hajin,
the tournament is next week, and we really need you to go there."
So, I asked him for a day to think about it, and finally decided to go.
Missing a few days of classes wouldn't be the end of the world, and
it would be cool to see Prague, an ancient capital of Europe.

## First Impression

I arrived at Prague airport around 10:30 p.m. Shops and restaurants
were closed and only a handful of people were walking around. As I
walked out of the airport gate, I found a young blonde girl holding a
white paper with my name on it. The girl was Klara, and she was there
with her mother. On the way to Klara's place, I could see Prague, dark
and calm beyond the car window. Even in the dark, I could see the
beauty of the city. At this moment, I knew that three and a half days
in Prague wouldn't be nearly enough.

## Czech Food

It's almost impossible to find any Czech food in Korea, so I was lucky
to try a few traditional Czech foods on this trip. I liked all the Czech
food I tried, but the most impressive one was SvÃŋÄŊkovÃ₄, which
had beef, mushrooms, and bread with a special cream sauce. It was so
delicious that I wanted to move to the Czech Republic just to have
it everyday. Well, maybe I am exaggerating a little bit. But anyway, I
hope I will have a chance to have this wonderful Czech food again
in the near future.

## Czech Go

The Korean Ambassador's Cup was attended by about 200 players. Most of them were Czech, but there were some strong players from other European countries as well. The playing venue was a huge hall with high ceilings inside a university campus. The place seemed much cooler than the KBA building to me.

As for my official activities, I played two rounds of simultaneous games and gave a public commentary of the final round. My teaching activities were all well-organized, and I got an impression that Czech Go players are experienced and skilled in handling Go events. I was also glad that the local people seemed excited to have me there for these few events.

I have a theory that Go players are all good people. Playing Go means one learns how to accept one's own mistakes and defeats, how to respect opponents and admit the fact that no one can win every time. Maybe I've just been lucky, but so far all Go players I've met have been pleasant and nice people to hang out with. The Czech players I met in Prague were very much so as well. They were friendly and welcoming. After the tournament, I went out with a group of young Czech players to a local pub, and we talked about baduk in Korea and the Czech Republic, music, art, literature, and so much more. I even sang a Korean song on a random street! It was such a fun evening.

## Sightseeing

Prague was full of breathtaking views and magnificent buildings. There were millions of tourists around the town, a testament to the city's fame. My sightseeing, however, was more special than an ordinary tour program because I was with Klara and Dominik. With these two local Go friends, I could really enjoy the city. The high view from the hills, colorful back alleys, a local basement restaurant with grey walls and dim light. All these things were possible thanks to them. On top of that, we had such sparkling conversations on so many subjects! Prague was an amazingly beautiful town, and I didn't want to go back to Korea.

## Looking back

I was feeling really tired by the time I arrived in Daejeon. I was hoping some terrible thing would happen to detain me in Prague, but unfortunately there was no such accident. Well, I guess I had to come back for school. Anyway, my trip to Prague was short but intense, and I will be missing this beautiful city until I can go back.

# Wishful Thinking

MAY 14$^{TH}$ 2010 — It took me a few days to recover from my trip to Prague, but now I am fully enjoying my school life again. These days I go to school early in the morning, and come home in the evening after dinner. Studying at the school library, reading at the café, hanging out with my school friends, attending the student reading club and special lectures are all fun, but still my favorite part of school life is taking classes.

Among the classes I am taking now, Critical Thinking has been especially interesting lately. In the last class, we talked about logical fallacies and rhetoric, and the concept of "wishful thinking" left a strong impression. This is because I received a question on my blog a while ago, and suddenly I realized how I wanted to answer the question while we were discussing wishful thinking in the class.

The question was as follows:

*When I'm playing lower kyus, sometimes I believe their groups are dead but they find a way to live. Often the answer wasn't difficult, but somehow I didn't see it. I'm starting to lose confidence in my ability to read in my games.*

When I first read this question, there were several anecdotes that came to my mind. I think the key point of the question was that this player is somehow influenced by the opponent's level. In baduk, there is a saying you should play the same no matter who your opponent is. Yet, it seems like many players (including myself when I was weaker) make mistakes in life & death situations when they are playing against a weaker player. I wasn't sure why this was the case, but I think I can explain it with wishful thinking.

According to an article I read, wishful thinking happens when people accept a claim simply because it would be pleasant if it were true (or unpleasant if it were false). In baduk, how often have you had thoughts like the following? First, you don't expect your opponent to see something that you yourself did not. Second, you believe you are able to capture your opponent's big group or save your own group in danger because you are "stronger" than your opponent. Third, you don't want to admit that your opponent, who is weaker than you, might outread you in life and death situations.

Another thing I would add is that your L&D skills are really up to you. Other areas of baduk, such as the opening, attacking or ko fights are relatively abstract because often there are multiple ways of playing depending on the surroundings and players' personal preferences. Consequently, a player's judgment could be influenced by teachers or books one studied with. In other words, your resources may be to blame for not improving in these areas. In L&D, however, there is only one answer, and the answer is the same regardless of players' styles. Plus, there are hundreds of problems available online that you can practice freely. Meaning, you can't really blame others for not getting better at it. So, beware of wishful thinking, and practice more L&D!

# Reunion With an Old Friend

June 2ND 2010 — It happened about a month ago, as I was walking back and forth at a supermarket. Since entering university, I discovered that I work better when I have snacks around. Blame my brain, I didn't choose this. Anyway, I was shopping for some snacks before getting to the big assignment that night, when I received a phone call from an unregistered number.

"Hello?"

"Hajin? It's me." A young man's voice, speaking Korean. Who was this? It sounded familiar, but I couldn't identify.

"Who?"

"It's me, Byoungjun."

"Byoungjun? REALLY? HEY! HOW HAVE YOU BEEN??"

Byoungjun and I studied baduk together in Daejeon under the same teacher when we were 7-9 years old. At 9, we both decided to move to Seoul for more serious training, and we ended up going to different baduk academies. A few years later, Byoungjun went to Japan, and now he is a Japanese professional player. Although we'd seen each other once in awhile when he came to Korea, usually for international tournaments, it was the first time that he called me from Japan.

"I am well. How are you? I am going to Korea! You are still in Daejeon, right? Can you come to Seoul on June 1st?"

"June 1st? Of course, I will come to Seoul to see you."

"Some Japanese pros are having a friendship baseball game with Korean pros on that day. Then there will be an after-party. You should come. Maeda-san is coming as well."

"I wouldn't miss it for the world! See you then!"

Later, he called me two more times to re-confirm that I was coming. June 1st was Tuesday, and my last class went until 4 o'clock. As soon as I was done at school, I ran to the train station. When I arrived at the restaurant around 7 p.m., a room full of pro players were having a great time with pork barbecue and beer. It was kind of funny to see them because most of them were red-faced after the baseball, soccer, and beer. There, I found Byoungjun, busily translating between Japanese and Korean.

Byoungjun told me 22 Japanese pros from Kansai Kiin came to Korea for this event. Thanks to Tygem, the sponsor, they were having a baseball game, a mini soccer league, after party, and friendship baduk matches the following day. Looking at how much these players were enjoying the beer, though, I could sense that the baduk matches wouldn't be too serious.

I was happy to catch up with Byoungjun. His case shows how difficult it is to become a pro in Korea, especially for men. He wasn't confident that he would pass the pro test in Korea, and that's why he decided to move to Japan while he was still young. He said he was doing alright in tournaments, but planning to go to a university in Osaka in a few years. I also told him that I was studying at an international university, and we were both glad to learn that both of us are doing well in our own ways.

I also had a chance to talk with other young Japanese pros. They were friendly and polite. With Byoungjun's translation, we talked about historical baduk figures, Korean and Japanese pop singers, popular TV shows, and so on. Just one problem was that there was a limit to our communication, since we had to rely on translation. It reminded me of when I went to Europe for the first time. I didn't speak much English then, and I was so frustrated. Yet, I am afraid I can't afford to start Japanese any time soon. I guess I will have to put it on my to-do list instead.

# Hajin's Baduk Formula

JUNE 13TH 2010 — With today's exam, I'm finished with math class! My official grade hasn't come up yet, but I am expecting either a B+ or an A, based on my assignments and midterm scores plus my feelings about the final exam today. As you may remember, I have been working really hard to catch up in math because I didn't study math in middle and high school.

I was really worried early this year that I might fail math and lose my scholarship. In order to maintain my scholarship, I had to get over 3.75/4.5 GPA. For your information, an A is 4.0 and a B+ is 3.5 in my school. So, I studied math 8 to 10 hours a day at home before the semester started, and continued to spend extra time on math throughout the semester. I also went to the math professor to ask for help, and my dad and sister were very helpful, too.

And, I did it! This feeling of achievement is incredible. Outside baduk, maybe English was my big strength, but English was never so intense for me. So, I've decided to celebrate my successful math career in a mathematical way. Here I've tried to express my hypothesis about improving baduk skills in mathematical terms! (Warning: this is for fun. It's not scientific or academic.)

$$V_g = (Q_s(T_s + Q_p))^{(T_g/(\text{Age}+L))}$$

- $V_g$: Speed in improving your baduk skills

- $Q_s$: Quality of sources (Teachers, books, playing partners)
  - 1 to 5 scale where 5 is extremely good

- $T_s$: Time of study
  - Average time you are investing a day (1 point for five minutes)

- $Q_p$: Quantity of playing
  - Average number of games you play a day (5 points per game)

- $T_g$: Natural Talent in Go
  - 1 to 5 scale where 5 is as talented as professionals

- Age: A player's current age.

- *L*: A player's current level of Go.

  - 1 to 30 scale where 7d is 30.

For example, if you are 30 years old and 2d, studying 30 minutes a day, playing one game a day with a moderate quality of books and partners. Given an average natural talent of 3, then, it would look like this!

$$(3(6+5))^{(3/(30+25))} = 48$$

You are improving at the speed of 48 per day :)

# World Cup

JUNE 27$^{\text{TH}}$ 2010 — I was sitting alone before a long table covered with a snow-white tablecloth. Shiny silver knives and forks were arranged in a graceful manner, and beautiful wine glasses were waiting for color to fill them in. A tall, brown-haired waiter in a black uniform walked in with a big white plate. The food seemed like pieces of bread and cheese. I suddenly felt very hungry. Should I wait for someone? Was I to eat here alone? The waiter was approaching. Three steps, two steps, one step, and now he was putting down the dish in front of me.

"WOAAAAAH!!!!"

I opened my eyes instantly. It was still dark. The clock was pointing at roughly 4 o'clock.

"It was a dream."

I murmured. Then, I remembered there was a World Cup game between Korea and Nigeria about this time. The Korean team must have scored a goal. I closed my eyes to get back to sleep, blaming the World Cup for interrupting my sweet dream. I felt a bit annoyed, thinking about my match in several hours, but then I realized my opponent's sleep must have been interrupted as well.

The World Cup is more popular than any other sporting event in Korea. Most Koreans wouldn't miss the Korean team's matches even if they weren't interested in soccer outside the World Cup. Moreover, millions of people will gather on streets, at parks or inside pubs to cheer and chant together. What makes the World cup different from other events? Thinking about it, I also wondered; will it be possible to have world baduk matches that are as popular as the World Cup someday?

Baduk and soccer have a few things in common. Two sides, strategies, and competition. Fun to watch and easy to take a side to root for. Also, soccer and baduk both take enough time for fans to enjoy beer and pizza while watching a game. Just like watching the end of a soccer match is more thrilling, watching baduk in countdown or overtime period is more exciting. In addition, you might make a friendly wager on the result with your friends. In this case baduk actually has an advantage because there is no chance of having a biased referee.

Of course, the differences are significant. Soccer requires teamwork while baduk is an individual effort. Soccer is easy to appreciate but you need to play baduk in order to enjoy watching other players' games. Not only that, baduk takes at least a few months for one to learn enough to start seeing what is happening in a game. Yet, does this mean baduk has no chance to become as popular? Well, something to think about, I guess.

# 2010 European Go Congress in Finland

AUGUST 5TH 2010 — I finished my semester with 4.4/4.5 GPA. I got an A in math, and A+ in all the other classes. When I saw my grades, though, I was more proud of the A than all the other A+s. Hours of math study seemed to have paid off well. My parents were happy that I made a smooth transition from pro player to college student, and I was relieved that I had secured my scholarship for the next semester.

Now that my semester was over, the KBA had plans for me. They were planning to send pros to several Go events in the West, and I was offered the spot to visit the European Go Congress and the Polish Summer Go Camp. It would have been nice if I could somehow connect the two trips to make it one, but due to the policies around overseas assignments, I am taking a short break in Korea in between. Maybe it's good that I can take this time to write about the European congress before I get busy with the Polish summer camp and the new semester.

This year's European Go Congress was hosted in Tampere, Finland. The best part of being in Finland was that the daylight lasted so long. At midnight it would get somewhat darker, but then it was bright again by 3 a.m. Thanks to this, I would often go out with other young Go players to wander around and party until late. Also, I liked how the air was so fresh and the weather wasn't too hot.

## Opening Ceremony

The opening ceremony was in a big cafeteria hall. An appetizing smell stimulated my empty stomach as I walked in. There were a few hundred people sitting or standing, and one Chinese gentleman was making a long speech with a translator beside him. He seemed like one of the sponsors. Though I have great respect for all sponsors, I was too distracted to listen to his speech then. I wanted to let organizers know we were there so they could introduce us to the audience. His speech was finally over, and the organizer said the dinner was ready. It turned out some other pros were arriving even later, and the organizers were planning to introduce all the pros at once the following day. So, I took a glass of wine and enjoyed the hot food.

## Game reviews

The first day I was sitting in the game review room, and no one came. I was a bit disappointed, but thought maybe people didn't have any interesting games yet. In my second day, I was sitting in the room alone again, wondering if anyone was going to show up. The room was getting warm as the afternoon sun was going high and strong. About 15 minutes after my review time started, one player passing by found me, and asked if I was there for game reviews. So I said he was correct, and he gladly walked in. Then the magic happened. Once we started reviewing, many other players came in, and eventually some of them left without a review because they had to wait for too long. This pattern continued until the last day I was there. I would get exhausted after hours of game reviews, but it was still better than sitting alone.

## Simultaneous Games

When Mr. Juho, the pro coordinator, asked us how many boards we wanted to play in our simul games, we just looked at each other. We were three pros from Korea, and we had simul games at the same time. Because no one was jumping in, I said, "eight?" Then one pro said to the other, "She is young, isn't she?" Playing simultaneous games is harder than it looks. It often causes back pain, headaches, and it drains your energy. That's why I say no when people ask me to play right after simul games. Nevertheless, playing simultaneous games is an important activity because it's a rare opportunity for local players to play with professionals. Coming back to the main story, we told Mr. Juho that we could have eight boards, but he ended up arranging five boards for each of us.

## Sightseeing

During the Congress I liked sitting outside. The weather was warm and fresh, and the peaceful atmosphere of Tampere was relaxing. I would be sitting under a tree or on a grass field, and once in awhile someone would approach for a chitchat. It was Tuesday afternoon, when I had just finished my game review session. I had about an hour to rest before the Pair-Go tournament, and I was heading for a tree to relax as usual. At the very moment, one man called me and asked if I had time for a game review. I hesitated. It wasn't that I didn't have the time. So after a few seconds of silence, I said, "Five minutes?" That's how I met him. Who? The one who gave me many useful tips about sightseeing in Tampere.

He couldn't remember the sequence of his game, and I asked him a few questions to avoid an awkward moment. That's how I found out he was a local player from Tampere. The following day was free for sightseeing, and I hadn't made any plans. So I asked him for recommendations on places and restaurants. He was so kind! We went to the registration desk to find a big map, and he pointed out many good places and restaurants considering location and price. Thanks to this lucky meeting, I had a wonderful sightseeing day with my friends. We even had a fancy but inexpensive lunch at a French restaurant in town.

Overall, my experience at the European Go Congress was a lot of fun, and I was happy that I could be there.

# Polish Summer Go Camp

AUGUST 30TH 2010 — After a week's break in Korea, I flew to Europe again to attend the Polish Summer Go Camp, also known (in Polish) as LSG. LSG is a two-week event in the Polish country-side. There were about 60 participants, and most of them were close friends with each other. I stayed at the camp for the full period as a lecturer and had one or two teaching activities every day during my stay.

### Journey to Alaska

The morning after my long flight to Poland, another big trip was waiting for me, from Warsaw to the Go camp venue, called "Alaska" (a Polish site not related to the U.S. state!). This time I was with two young brothers, Cezary and Mariusz. Three of us sat in a compartment of an old train. It was a hot, sunny day. There was a dial for the air conditioner, but it didn't work. So we opened a window. With fresh air it felt way better, but we had to withstand serious noise. Thus, for four and a half hours on the train, we kept bothering the old window, opening and closing it. In the meantime, we distracted ourselves by talking about the Go community and playing Go on a small magnetic set.

The second train was worse. We transferred to it in a small town, and all the seats were already taken. At first we stood in a corner beside an exit, but soon sat on the floor out of exhaustion. This train was older and slower. The air was hot, and our position was uncomfortable. I was feeling tired from the long trip and fell asleep.

About two hours later, we arrived at the last station of the train. Our trip wasn't over though. There, Kangur and Kamyk were waiting to give us a ride. Along the way, I enjoyed the view of endless green and golden fields out the window. That was my first impression of Poland. Rich in nature, and natural in living.

### First day in Alaska

Alaska reminded me of a small square of a farmers' village. A tall wooden totem was at the center of the square with a yellow direction board and two large logs, on which about three people could sit and talk. Beside the totem place, there was a main street that connected all the buildings in Alaska. Along the street, you found a big wooden table with long, flat chairs. This was a great place to play baduk under the sun. All the buildings were around there: a corner shop where you can get beer, the kitchen, the Sun house (main building), the washing place, cottages, and the playing and dining hall. It doesn't sound like much, but I didn't really need anything else.

As a part of the tour, I followed a group of young fellows through a forest.. Soon, the lake unfolded before my eyes. It was so peaceful with the forest around it. On the small beach by the lake there were tall swings, and a wooden dock that extended to the lake for diving and sitting. I sat on the road and put my legs into the lake. Cold and fresh. Some people greeted me and welcomed me there. So I smiled back at them.

At dusk, a campfire was set up. Packs of sausages, bread, and long iron skewers were prepared as well. Although I'm not a big sausage fan, this campfire was like a fairy tale. To make it even more charming, one young man offered to hold my skewer for me, because you needed to stand really close by the fire in order to cook the sausage. What chivalry! At last I got my sausage on a white paper plate, and it seemed better than an expensive steak on a porcelain dish. Of course, there was cold Polish beer to make everything better.

Soon enough it became dark all around. So dark that you could barely see one step ahead. The sky was breathtaking. Thousands of stars were glowing. Field, forest, lake, fire, and stars; all these things were just overwhelming. I was happy to feel nature so close, and wished I had this opportunity more often.

## Lake

I can't imagine Alaska without the lake. Although the lake is not visible directly from the main area, the beach of the lake is an iconic place. Like a ritual, everyone went there at least once a day. It was definitely the best place to relax, read a book, play Baduk, drink beer, or swim, if you can.

Swimming seemed so easy when other people showed me, but it didn't work for me. I would repeat in my head, 'legs, arms, breath, legs, arms, breath…' then sank. Sigh. There was another problem, besides me being un-athletic: I had different teachers each time, and they each taught different methods. This reminded me of the time I had more than one baduk teacher. It was good to learn different styles, but there were times that one teacher would say exactly the opposite of the other. It confused me then, but now I understand there can be more than one answer. If swimming is the same, I guess

I will understand when I get much better. At that moment, though, I was only confused and unable to swim.

## Lecture

For a group of players with a wide range of levels, game reviews are perfect lecture material. Reviews cover all the stages of a game, and it's easy to find something to learn regardless of skill level. One problem with reviewing, however, is that showing one's own games in front of everyone could be scary. Actually, as a young student, I also avoided my teacher's eyes when he was looking for a game to review.

When I discussed lectures at LSG with Tasuki, an organizer of the camp, we agreed to have game reviews, but we were concerned that there might be no volunteers. Thus, he asked me to bring some of my games just in case. It was a wise choice. The majority of my lectures were the attendees' game reviews, but I also ended up giving three full lectures on my own games. If someone attended all three lectures, they would know about me better than anyone else, for I'd never introduced six of my games to the same audience.

## Simultaneous Games

Although I have played so many simultaneous games since I became pro, I didn't know there were different ways of playing simul games. Thus, when Tasuki asked "Do you mind playing a simul with Jun, Fisz, and me?" I didn't exactly know what he meant. So, I said, "No, I don't." I assumed we would play at the same time. However, it turned out he literally meant 'with' – as in partners. The four of us shared 18 boards, walking around. It was really different, and fun.

Here is one secret. People get nervous when they play a professional player at simultaneous games. Many of them have never played a pro before, and have no idea how strong their opponent will be. On the other hand, pro players usually seem calm. Yet, I also get nervous when I play simul games. Why? Because I don't know how strong my opponents will be either. For pro players, there is nothing worse than losing respect. One day, I was playing simultaneous games against eight players. They were all surprisingly good at the opening, and I got scared that I would lose every game. At the time, I was thinking "Goodness, why did I give them so many handicaps? I can't lose them all. What should I do?" Well, eventually I managed to win six games that day, but it was hard.

## Phantom Go

Do you know what Phantom Go is? It seemed well-known among Polish players. Is it also known in other countries? I haven't heard of it in Korea though. In Phantom Go, you don't know where your opponent played. Instead, the referee would tell you that there is your opponent's stone if you play on the same place. It seems unbelievably good in the opening, since you only see your own stones. As you find your opponent's stones, however, you realize the situation isn't so good after all. While playing this game I felt so stupid. I couldn't play the knight's move, the diagonal move or the one space jump. At first I used them out of habit, but soon I learned they had been cut off, and one entire corner was destroyed. Then, I managed to lose another corner. A lesson from this game: It's a gift to see where your opponent has played.

## Coming back

Other than playing or teaching Go, I also enjoyed hanging out with the Polish players. I learned how to play volleyball, tried horseback riding, went on an adventure through the forest with a few other players, and enjoyed their nightly parties with beer. It was a rich and memorable experience, and I highly recommend this camp to any Go players looking for a relaxing summer Go holiday.

# Lee Sedol 9p's Commentary Books

SEPTEMBER 29TH 2010 — A new semester started as September began, and once more I transformed back from a professional player to a college student. My second semester is going as smoothly as I hoped, and I am very happy with my classes and activities. Compared with studying baduk at a high level, I feel studying business at school is easy. Professors, textbooks, the Internet or my classmates can answer my questions, and I often find real-life business examples around me. In baduk, it's difficult to get a quality book in the first place, and even harder to find someone to answer my questions.

Today, I read a news article about Lee Sedol 9-dan's commentary books that just came out. Lee Sedol 9-dan has been one of the top players in the world for the last few years and is highly regarded for his genius at reading. According to the article, Lee chose the nine most meaningful games of his career and discussed them in great detail with his sister, Lee Sena, a writer and a strong amateur player. She recorded their discussions with a video camera and wrote them down in three volumes, three games per book. I was amazed at this description because I koew that most commentary books on top players were written by either a strong amateur or a professional player with writing skills, with the top player himself proofreading at the end. Yet, this process seemed to have recorded Lee Sedol 9-dan's thoughts as accurately as possible.

Also, Lee Sedol 9-dan's book reminded me of *The Prince*, the book written by Niccolo Machiavelli. Machiavelli was an Italian diplomat and a writer in the 16th century. In the "Dedication" of the book in the very beginning, Machiavelli writes that he was looking for the most precious thing to bring to his Prince. He decided that among his possessions there was nothing more valuable than his knowledge and experience as a diplomat. Thus, he took hours and hours of contemplation and study to write this short book as a gift to the Prince. In other words, the book was written by a great scholar, who sincerely wanted to deliver his knowledge to the Prince. Machiavelli's advice may not be relevant in today's world anymore, but I still felt excited to read this priceless book.

Machiavelli and Lee Sedol 9-dan are both great gifts for the world in their own areas, and I believe we are so fortunate that they produced books. So, as I read Machiavelli's book in Korean, I hope the Western players will be able to read Lee Sedol 9-dan's books in their own languages soon. Also, if there is no plan for the translation yet, I would be more than happy to do the job. Though I am busy with my study and part time work, it would be such an honor to translate the *Prince* of my own field.

# My Theory on How I Won

NOVEMBER 5TH 2010 — I have a surprising update: I won the final round of the preliminary tournament today[6] and qualified for the Korean team for the Jeong-kwan-jang Cup, an annual women's team competition among Korea, China and Japan. Each team has five players: the KBA selects four pros in a preliminary tournament, and the last player is recommended by the sponsor. This competition offers bigger prize money than any other women's tournament and receives the most media attention. Thus, many female players' top objective is to join this national team, and I've just passed the qualification tournament for the 4th time.

You may wonder how I made it despite all the distractions; studying at a university, teaching trips to Europe, blog entries, and so on. Frankly speaking, even I didn't expect to pass the preliminary, since I've made the choice to do other things with my life. The decision was not easy, but I've been committed to it. Rather than juggling both worlds, I've been focusing on my study at school while maintaining my baduk career at a minimum level. In fact, I wouldn't have

---

[6] Appendix: ○ Lee Hajin – Lee Jihyun ●

participated in the preliminary tournament if it hadn't been held right after my midterm exams, when I could take a few days off from school without disrupting my studies.

As I was playing in this tournament, I realized that my life changes have affected my attitude toward baduk as well. First, I take more risks. When I see an interesting move and a proper move, I've begun to choose the interesting one. Before, I feared losing so much that I couldn't possibly choose uncertain moves over what I knew to be safe. Now, I am not desperate to survive in tournaments anymore, and free to experiment. Second, I enjoy playing again. Though I got into the game because I liked it so much, at some point baduk became difficult and exhausting. I didn't want to leave it, but at the same time I often dreamed about escaping from it. When I played these preliminaries, though, I really enjoyed playing itself. Apart from anything else, it was just fun to play. I am not sure how these changed my play, but there must have been something different.

My theory is that these changes confused my opponents, who thought they knew me or my playing style. Also, I am probably at the point where my baduk skill is benefiting from my new experiences but hasn't suffered yet from lack of practice. So, though I am excited I won today, I don't expect this level of performance to last. I have set my direction away from baduk, and I am confident in my decision.

## Trip to Hong Kong

FEBRUARY 23<sup>RD</sup> 2011 — I finished my second semester successfully, but I wasn't as successful in my match against the Chinese player for the team competition. I apologized to my teammates that I couldn't contribute to the team, but at least I did my best.

In the meantime, I received a surprising gift from my school. Six students were selected to be offered a study trip to Hong Kong, and my name was on the list! In the last two semesters, I took 12 classes and received 10 "A+"s and 2 "A"s, so I guess that helped. The purpose of the trip was to take a 40-hour "Effective Professional Communication in English" course over two weeks at Hong Kong Polytechnic University, and my school paid for all expenses. Another great thing was that my best friend, Wanna, was also selected as one of the six students.

Everything went well. Our room was decent, classes were interesting, and the weather was warm and pleasant. We had classes until 3 p.m. and went sightseeing until late at night. Wanna and I visited many places around Hong Kong and went to Macau on our free day. Yet what I really learned from this trip was from none of these. Rather, the lesson was from several misbehaving students who partied overnight and came to classes late. One morning Wanna and I met them at breakfast, and they proudly told us that they were coming straight from a party. Also, one of them made fun of me for saying I was planning to go to a public library after class. These students were not from my school, but were taking the same course as we were. Their behavior was not my business, but somehow it really bothered me.

Observing them, I realized that traveling can be like living in a dream for some people. They overspend, drink too much or do irresponsible things because they feel everything will go back to normal when they go back. They are physically and mentally far from the reality where they came from. Yet what is traveling for? What do you want to see about the place you are visiting? If you live a dream, you would only see the illusion of the place. The illusion that businesses have built for tourists. We should remember that the place we visit is a real world for the local people. It's someone's hometown, neighborhood or workplace just like ours, in our world.

I want traveling to integrate with my life as if it were continuing seamlessly. If I go as a student, I will be in the classroom. If I am invited as a professional player, I will focus on the event while it's happening. I want to be myself, and that seems to be a real way to experience the place. Why shouldn't I go to a library when I like going to libraries? Is it really important that the library is not the best-known destination in the region? Should I go shopping just because it's the world's popular place for shopping, even though I have no interest in it?

Playing baduk is just like that. The opponent, the stakes of the game, the equipment, the environment, or the location of the game may change, but you should stay true to yourself and focus on what you are good at.

Looking back, the Hong Kong trip was a big lesson. There was no reason why I should be bothered by other students' problems, but it still brought my mood down. Then I came to think about traveling in general. Some may say that traveling is an opportunity to be someone else in a strange world. I would say, however, that I want my trips to be natural and real. The taste could be sweet, sour, or anything else, but I want them to be as they are meant to be.

## Insecurities

APRIL 7TH 2011 — The winter vacation passed by like the wind, especially with my venture in Hong Kong and the main round of the Jeong-kwan-jang Cup. I haven't made an entry about the match[7] because I was sad that I didn't manage to win, but that's tournament life. I do my best and accept the result. Anyway, now that the weather is getting warmer, I am back at school as a sophomore.

Something I like about studying business is that there are so many interesting books I can read outside of textbooks. The other day, I read a book titled *Straight from the Gut*, written by Jack Welch, the former CEO of General Electric. There were many interesting stories and lessons regarding his business philosophy and strategy, but somehow it was his personal confessions that I kept thinking of again and again.

---

[7] Appendix: ○ Lee Hajin – Rui Naiwei ●

In his book, he writes, "Outwardly, I had a pretty good dose of self-confidence, and those who knew me would have described me as self-assured, cocky, decisive, quick and tough. Inwardly, I still had plenty of insecurities." I understand that everyone has a certain degree of insecurities. Yet, it just didn't feel real that someone like Jack Welch had insecurities like everyone else. Then I wondered. What were his insecurities? What are mine?

Lee Sedol, Gu Li, and several other top players always look so calm. They may speak humbly in public, but their expressions and gestures would suggest that they are confident. Yet, I imagine they have their own insecurities as well. I've never thought about it seriously, but after some reflection, I noticed two areas where I am insecure.

## Baduk skills

My first insecurity is about losing, or losing terribly. Losing a match is one thing, and it's terrible by itself, but it becomes much worse when I am unhappy with my performance. If I put it simply, the words that would hurt me the most are, "You are not as strong as I expected" or "I guess pros are not that much stronger than amateurs, judging by your play." Whenever I played, I was at a certain risk of hearing this kind of comments, and I often avoided playing at all outside professional matches and unofficial young pros' leagues.

It's ironic that I am insecure about my baduk skills when I am stronger than most people in the world. Yet, people still judge even when they themselves are not any better. When my baduk skills are criticized, I feel my whole life is being criticized and there is nothing good I can do. Rationally I know this is not true, but it's hard to change how I feel about it.

In the olden days, the top pros used to say "I would like to make a good kifu (game record)," when they were asked about upcoming matches. When I was young, I thought nothing could be more boring. Don't we play to win? Who cares the quality of the game?

Having experience as a professional player myself, however, I realized that playing poorly hurts my pride more than just losing the game. In addition, focusing on playing a good game rather than winning is actually better for my performance. All I should do is try to find the best move each time, and if I do well in that, I will win.

## Appearance

In my youth, I was often told, "You are not pretty, but you are smart." I think it was meant to be a compliment by emphasizing the latter, but at some point I came to believe it in my heart, and became shy around mirrors and cameras. Then, there was a guy that I liked when I was 15 years old. He heard somewhere that I was interested in him and told me I wasn't pretty enough for him. I was embarrassed and annoyed because I didn't even ask to be his girlfriend. Somehow I wasn't surprised, though. I was upset, but deep inside I thought he wasn't wrong.

Insecurity is a strange thing. I would say things like, "I know I am not pretty" as if I didn't care, but if someone replied, "Yeah, you're not pretty", it would hurt my feelings. A hundred times, I've convinced myself that looking pretty was not what I value nor what I prioritize, but somehow I still can't help feeling insecure about it.

So, I think these two areas are the main sources of my insecurities. Yet, as I grow older, I hope I will become more comfortable about them.

# Professional Status

MAY 1ST 2011 — Yesterday, I had an interesting conversation over dinner about being a professional baduk player. My companions were two gentlemen, one from the US and the other from the UK. In the West, "professional" indicates a full-time, paid job. Also, no matter how skilled you are, you are considered an amateur player as long as you don't get paid for it. Concerning players who have other jobs but still play as a part-time job, people would call them "semi-professional". It's clearer if you think about the origin of the words. The word "professional" stems from "profess," which means it's what you have to admit to doing – it's your job. On the other hand, the "amateur" comes from the Latin "amatus," meaning "love" or "having been loved."

One example my friends used was professional tennis players. Tennis players don't have a special qualifying test to become professional, but they would be considered professional if they performed in major matches and got paid for them. If they stopped playing actively, however, they would be considered either as semi-professional or as a retired professional. Also, the players who teach as a full-time job might be considered "professionals" even if they don't perform in tournaments.

Baduk is different. Being a professional player in Korea, Japan, China or Chinese Taipei, is more like having a degree, like a Ph.D. First, it comes with honor and prestige. Once you become a professional player, you keep the title of "professional" until you decide to retire. Yet, since there is no reason to retire early, it is safe to say that one is a professional for life. In fact, no player retires unless they have a special reason, like if they become too weak, physically, to go to the tournament venue.

Just like any other policy, the unique professional system of baduk has both good and bad sides. On the bright side, it makes it highly desirable to become a professional player. Though the income may not be stable, the status is secure. Also, it allows professional players to explore other paths. You can see my case, for example: If I had to give up the professional status, I doubt I would have dared to become a college student. Thanks to the current system, though, I could choose to pursue other things. Now, I don't make much money from playing, but my professional title is as secure as before.

However, if you look at this from the baduk fans' point of view, this system lets the professional world stagnate. Because players retire so late, the KBA can only afford to accept a limited number of new professional players each year. It's true that Korean pros are strong because of the hard competition to become pro, but on the other hand it's a great loss when young and talented players spend their prime time trying to become professional when they could grow faster if they were already competing with other pros. In addition, many prodigies, who are as strong as many existing professional players, can still fail to become pro after several years of intensive study. This both dilutes the competitiveness of professional tournaments and takes away places from "purely amateur players" in most amateur tournaments.

I like that my professional title is secure, but I believe the current system is not sustainable. I don't know when or if this system will change. If it does, though, I don't think we should blindly copy what tennis or other sports do. We need our own policies that reflect our culture and characteristics and at the same time allow the baduk community to grow in the new era.

## Expectation Magic

MAY 16<sup>TH</sup> 2011 — My life as a student is busy but peaceful at the same time. I mean, I have a lot of activities going on, but they are never high pressure or stressful. Many of them are volunteer activities and I am happy to do them. As a professional player, I was never busy but always somewhat stressed.

It seems like university is a good place to think about ourselves. Maybe it's because we often make directional choices for our lives while we are in university. For most of my life, I had only one direction in mind, and that was to pursue a career in tournament baduk. Yet, now I am studying at a university and need to decide my direction again. Where should I go? Then, I had these following questions:

Who am I? What am I doing here? What do I want to do in the future? What are my strengths? What makes me happy? What makes me frustrated? Why?

Since I became an university student, I found myself asking those questions often. My identity was confusing because I had left something I worked on for my whole life. I am a professional baduk player, but I rarely play in tournaments anymore. I also wondered about my feelings. If I don't know why I want what I want, who else would know? It seemed, though, that I didn't know about myself very well. That's probably why sages like Socrates or Lao Tzu taught the importance of knowing oneself.

Among the pool of philosophical questions, I was thinking about my feelings today. What makes me happy and why? Or on the opposite side, what makes me sad or frustrated? How do they do that to me? Though I believe frustration and sadness have their own value, such as adding more depth to my character, I still looked for an answer as an alchemist might seek the perfect formula. If I can understand the causes, wouldn't it be easier to deal with them? Then, I found a magical element that was behind almost all my feelings.

You may know it already. It's my expectations. I realized that I was happy to be with my boyfriend for two hours if I had been expecting to have less than two hours. However, I would be sad with two hours if I thought I would have more time than that. I was disappointed to get a 91/100 on my Marketing exam because I thought my answers were perfect, but I was quite satisfied with my 25/30 in Statistics exam because the exam was insanely difficult. It's like expectations are magic. Everything is relative, and they are evaluated by my arbitrary standard that I unconsciously set in my head.

Expectations influence baduk players as well. I noticed that when players expect to lose, their moves somehow lack fighting spirit. When they expect to win, however, they don't give up easily on the game. Also, players often feel proud of themselves when they do better than they expected rather than based on any specific results. Then, I ran into this paradox: I need to keep my expectations low in order to avoid being frustrated, but I should expect to win when I am playing so that I would fight hard. In addition, I would be lying to myself if I set my expectations lower than what I know I can do, or if I expected to win when there was little reason to believe so.

I thought I found a magic bullet that would make me happy all the time, or at least avoid being frustrated. Yet, it seems like there isn't much I can do with it. I guess the best thing to do is to be honest and fair with myself. This may sound obvious to you, but actually I am good at making up excuses, rationalizing my reasons, or relying on luck more than I should. So, rather than trying to cleverly manipulate my expectations, I decided to see myself as I am, other people as they are, and the world as it is, as objectively as possible. I haven't practiced this much yet, but I have good feelings about it!

## Music and Stories

JUNE 9ᵀᴴ 2011 — I love taking classes at my school, and each class is special. This semester I chose a music class for elective credits, and I couldn't be happier with my choice. Our professor, Ms. Hae-eun Kim, was a cellist who studied music at Juilliard and Yale. She was enthusiastic and confident in her expressions, and introduced us to different corners of music each week. What a pity that today was the last class already!

In the first class, Professor Kim asked, "Why did you come to this class?" The whole class fell into silence. She was looking at us, waiting. The tension was stifling. Music... Why did I register for a music class? The question was so simple, but my mind was all foggy. "I like classical music, and wanted to know more about it." My answer broke the ice and invited other classmates to talk. Yet, I was still thinking there was something more. I tried to find the answer for a bit longer, but soon I was distracted by other classmates' answers and Ms. Kim's comments.

Later on, I realized it was exploration and new experiences that I was hoping to find here. Music is a new world to me. I registered for the class not knowing what to expect. It was an adventure. Turned out, music became my favorite class of the semester. I was always excited to go to the music class and never felt sleepy even when I was tired. The class was from 9 a.m. to noon, Fridays, and many students would fall asleep listening to classical music.

Learning about all the beautiful music, rules, history, and different instruments was great. But, more than that, I learned the power of stories. It amazed me how much difference it made in my mind when there was a story associated with a certain musician or a piece of music. For example, once I learned more about Andrea Bocelli, I couldn't listen to his songs without feeling sad. His voice was deep and emotional, and I would imagine what it's like to live in darkness.

Another example was "Cirque du Soleil." Though I heard of the name before, I had no idea what they were about. I was never interested in circuses, and I assumed they were just a modern circus. I was so wrong. Cirque du Soleil is a comprehensive stage art. The levels of acrobatics, music, choreography, costumes and stage organization were all amazing, and they would be beautifully presented through one story. It was fascinating to see how having a story changed a circus so dramatically.

Someday, I would like to bring more story elements into the professional baduk scene as well. We do have professional players' interviews and such, but I feel it's not enough. When baduk fans learn more about the players and tournaments at a more intimate level, they will be able to enjoy the games at a different level.

# Graduation Ceremony

JUNE 13TH 2011 — There was a graduation ceremony today. Of course I am still far from graduating, but it was officially the last day for my best friend, Wanna. I wore the nicest dress in my closet and got a nice flower bouquet, a small gift and a congratulation card. On the way to the school, I told myself that I would enjoy the ceremony – touching speeches and all. The auditorium was crowded with familiar faces in black gowns and caps. I knew it was a happy day for them. I knew I would see them again someday. I knew it was nothing new, but a life event that happens all the time. Despite all that, I couldn't stop my tears, thinking Wanna was leaving.

Though it's been only a year and a half, she's been much more than a friend. I called her my big sister, and that was how I felt about her. We entered SolBridge at the same time, and shared a dorm room in our first semester. From the second semester on, I stayed with my family and Wanna moved to a single studio outside the dorm because only the first semester had a dormitory requirement. I really wanted to stay with Wanna, but economically it was better to stay with my family.

Our school's MBA program is two years, but Wanna is graduating after her third semester. It didn't surprise me that she was graduating early, though. After all, that's how we became so connected in the first place. We were both dedicated students. Neither of us was interested in parties or shopping, but we would study together and discuss our classes, culture, books, and so on. She would listen to my life stories, tell me about hers, cook Thai food for us, and visit my family for dinner once in a while. I loved spending time with her. Yet, she was going back to her home country, Thailand, soon after the ceremony.

Before SolBridge, all my friends were baduk players, and I haven't really worried about losing them. I met most of them when we were much younger. We went through a difficult time together in our race to become pro, and regardless of whether they succeeded or not, we were all still connected through baduk. In fact, I did have one non-baduk player friend a long time ago, but that didn't go well.

It was in my first year in middle school. We were from the same elementary school, but we became really close in middle school. She didn't talk much, but had a bright smile and kindness. We always had lunch together, and she helped me catch up with the afternoon classes and homework when I left school after lunch to study baduk. It was an arrangement made between my baduk teacher and the principal of the school for my baduk training. Missing almost half of school life was not fun. Imagine watching only the first half of each episode in a TV series. You would still understand what's going on, but miss the details that make the show interesting. Yet, my friend was so caring and helpful that I could still enjoy school life.

A few months later, however, I started noticing that she was somehow avoiding me to hang out with other students. At first I thought I was being oversensitive, but eventually I asked her if I'd done anything wrong. She hesitated, then said she couldn't stand any more that her only friend would leave school after lunch, and she was alone the whole afternoon on. I felt like the worst person in the world. I couldn't believe that I'd never thought about her once I left the school. Since that event, I'd decided not to have any close friends at school.

Since then, Wanna was my first close friend outside baduk. Thinking about my relationships with baduk players and non-baduk players, I realized that baduk players' relationships were generally different from those of non-players. Baduk players don't experience changes in schools, majors, graduations, teachers and so on. Instead, we have the same teacher and same peers for years, with rare occasions to deal with new people. In addition, there are certain typical qualities of baduk players: They are often independent and quiet. When you're a baduk player, you are the captain. You make all decisions alone and take responsibility for the outcome. No discussions, and no blaming others.

Yet, coming to SolBridge, I met a lot of new people and worked in teams. Now my best friend is moving on with her life, and I will have to keep in touch with her since there is nothing like baduk to connect us. I can't help feeling sad about Wanna[8]'s leaving, but I am also lucky to have had these life experiences!

---

[8] Wanna is back in Thailand, teaching in university. We are still close friends!

# Part IV
# *Management in Go*

## The Tipping Point of Baduk

July 1ST 2011 — Another semester ended soon after Wanna's graduation ceremony. I am taking a couple summer classes for extra credits these days, while taking things easy and reading a lot of books outside class. Then, later this month I will be visiting California to attend the US Go Congress.

I just finished reading an interesting book called *The Tipping Point*. It's a sociological book by Malcolm Gladwell, who also wrote *Blink* and *Outliers*. As the title implies, *The Tipping Point* analyzes the causes, components and processes of social epidemics, using diverse examples such as fashions, TV programs, diseases, etc. Through those cases, the author presents what happened, why and what lessons can be taken from them.

I got *The Tipping Point* for my study in business. As I was reading the book, however, my baduk playing self poked her head out to show interest in the topic. The book was whispering, *"Let me tell you the secrets of popularity."* Does that mean anything can tip? Can baduk, too, tip and gain worldwide popularity?

According to the book, there are three important elements in sparking a lasting social epidemic: The law of of the few, the stickiness factor and the power of context. Let me go over them one-by-one and see if baduk may use these to tip.

The law of the few suggests that it's more important to target only a few influential people who matter in spreading popularity. In other words, it's not how many people you convinced that counts – the question is whether you convinced certain types of influential people who will transfer the message to the public in their own ways. When the public gets a message from these people, the message becomes more powerful and convincing. I am not sure if we can or should seek out these people specifically, but it would certainly help to bear this research in mind when promoting baduk.

The stickiness factor is a quality that makes an idea remain in people's minds, and possibly influence them in the future. The book introduces techniques for increasing the stickiness of an idea through the examples of *Sesame Street* and *Blue's Clues* – children's TV programs. Reading this part of the book, I had two ideas. One is a TV version of a children's baduk program. Just as *Sesame Street* was designed to be entertaining and also educational, this TV program could be made to be fun, while teaching baduk in a friendly way.

The second idea is to develop a manual for teachers. Looking at the extensive research and experiments those successful TV programs conducted, I thought the same rigor and analysis was necessary for baduk education and promotion. For instance, we might have a conference for baduk instructors to discuss teaching beginners and how to make baduk stickier for the learners. Scholars reveal their academic findings, and instructors would share their experiences and know-how. After the conference, we publish a manual on how to teach beginners depending on their cultural backgrounds or age groups. Through categorizing the learners, educators could tailor their techniques to be the stickiest possible for the students.

The third element is the power of context. The power of an idea to tip is dependent on the time and place it emerges. Korea has probably the best context in the world for baduk players. Virtually all

Korean people know what baduk is, even if they don't know how to play. Many of them perceive the game as smart person's hobby, and agree that it has educational value for children. Occasionally, you find people playing in parks, and there are two university departments and two cable TV stations fully devoted to baduk. Then, what can or should other countries do to set up such a powerful context for baduk?

The author suggests that groups and communities help. In the case of baduk, national associations, regional clubs and school clubs would be the groups that may fuel the spread of the game. When the groups settle, they also need to grow by welcoming beginners and motivating members with events, such as friendship matches between nations, regions or schools.

Working to tip baduk into a worldwide epidemic may require a great deal of resources without immediate payback. Also, there is a question of who should take which part, or how to work together. If we do get to work on it, though, I think reviewing the principles and ideas from this book will be a good first step!

# Nightmares

JULY 23RD 2011 — The weather has been really hot, and I've been mostly spending my time at cafés. Cafés are great for studying or working, though sometimes I feel bad about taking their table for hours and hours over a cup of coffee. Yet, I think café owners expect this from the beginning, don't they? Anyway, today was an exception because I stayed home feeling tired. My sleep was disrupted by a nightmare last night.

Since I was small, I was far from being sensitive – I slept well anywhere, any time. Once in a while, though, I had nightmares. I would dream about losing matches; the final round of a tournament, an important game in an Insei league or the last game to pass the pro qualification.

After I became a professional player I stopped dreaming about losing games. I am still stressed and discouraged by defeats, but the pressure is much lighter. The best part of being a professional player is that your status is secure, and you always have a new tournament to attend. Then, another kind of nightmare started bothering me. Living in a small place in Seoul by myself, I was often worried about security. My place was on a rooftop of a 4-story building, and once anyone climbed the building, it would be easy to walk into my room. In my dreams, strange men would break into my place, and I would wake up frightened and panicked.

Two years ago, I moved to my parents' place in Daejeon. Living with my family was very comfortable and I stopped having nightmares for a while. From the beginning of this year, however, a new kind of nightmare began visiting me. In the new nightmares, I would forget to go to a class, mess up an exam, and end up getting an F. It might sound mild compared to my previous nightmares, but they still made me frightened and disturbed my sleep. Luckily my GPA so far is the opposite of an F.

A few days ago, I had an interesting nightmare. The dream was fragmentary, but the pieces were somehow connected. At first, I was in a classroom, and everything seemed normal. Then I was playing a match. I don't remember which tournament or who my opponent was, but I was playing terribly – so badly that I was horrified by my own moves. Yet, I couldn't stop making bad moves and had to watch helplessly as I lost the game. At some point I was back at the school. It was the same classroom, but something was different. Everyone there seemed mad at me. The professor, about whom I don't remember anything, asked me a few questions. I was silent, not knowing how to answer. He said I got an F.

My bad dream says I am afraid of failing in both fields. Yet, I know what I want. I am not giving up on it because I am afraid, or my dreams say I am afraid. My aspiration is to explore, experience, and later bring something to the baduk community that no other player can. Despite my bad dreams, I became a professional player. In the face of those nightmares, I got A's in most of my classes. I am not worried. Whatever my nightmares say, I know that they are only showing me what is important. These goals are too valuable to give up because of my fears. I will live my dreams, not my nightmares.

# US Go Congress in Santa Barbara

AUGUST 21ST 2011 — It's most college students' dream to travel abroad during summer vacation. I am so lucky to be a professional player and get a free trip to the US for teaching baduk at the Go Congress! Though I don't get to do too much sightseeing, I enjoy hanging out with Go players and helping them see better moves. Since the KBA confirmed that they were sending me and another pro to the US Go Congress, I've been eagerly waiting for the date and it finally came.

### Journey to the US

On the morning of July 27th, Korea was suffering under a severe rainstorm which caused mudslides and floods in many cities. Daejeon wasn't affected much, but Seo 9p, the other pro sent by the KBA, had to come to the airport by taxi because the airport bus stopped operating due to the heavy rains. I was worried that our flight would be delayed, but we took off on time and safely arrived in LA.

### The Congress site

Santa Barbara was small and beautiful. Buildings were sitting like ladies with dark orange hair and soft apricot dresses. Tall palm trees shielded sunlight and smiled to welcome. Colorful flowers chit-chatted with bees and butterflies, and grizzled streets yawned as if they didn't care whether their territory was taken or not.

Andy Okun, president of the American Go Association, told me that the Congress committee originally planned to book the UCLA campus. Yet, UCLA was too expensive while UCSB was a lot more reasonable. Though UCLA would have been a convenient location, I liked Santa Barbara a lot. It's beautiful, and the campus was right by the beach. I was surprised that the campus was full of students already, because two years ago when the Congress was held at George Mason University, the campus was almost empty aside from the Congress participants. Later I heard that UCSB is popular for summer classes and camps.

## Lectures

Unlike my first Congress, in which I was assigned 12 simultaneous games out of 12 official activities, this year I received six lectures, three commentaries and three simultaneous games. I was happy to see this because I prefer lectures and commentaries. They are more interactive and fun. Having lectures in front of many people was exciting and stressful at the same time. I tried to be confident, but couldn't be sure if I would satisfy my audience's expectations. Thankfully some of them came to me to say they liked my lectures, and I felt relieved to hear that.

## Pair-Go

On Tuesday, there was a Pair-Go tournament in the evening. I thought I couldn't play because I had a commentary scheduled at the same time, but Lisa [9] told me she could easily move my schedule to some other time. So I made a last minute proposal to Matthew, a strong player I had known for some time, and he kindly agreed to play with me.

Playing Pair-Go is very interesting, especially when you play sudden-death (no countdown). You don't want to spend too much

---

[9] the Congress Director

time, but you also don't want to make mistakes. We had some tough situations because of the time, but we managed to win both games! I wonder if having known each other for some years helped. Anyway, I once again won the first board, and remained undefeated in the US Pair-Go Open.

## Off-day

Wednesday was the off-day. Ever since I arrived in Santa Barbara, I was looking for something fun and interesting to do for the free day. Universal Studio or Disneyland seemed a bit costly, and the winery tour was already familiar to me. I tried horseback riding in Poland, and the Channel Islands were too far for a day trip. One day, I noticed a trip to Santa Barbara downtown for their "August Days Festival." It was an old Spanish culture festival where you can find Spanish handcrafts, costumes and street foods. Nothing could sound better than this!

Good company, sunny weather, and beautiful streets – everything was exactly how I would want it to be for a holiday. The festival touched the downtown like a wand of a happy witch, and made whole streets lively and cheerful. We had iced coffee next to a painting of David Alfaro Siqueiros, and wandered around the magical streets. We had a Hawaiian lunch and ice cream while we watched some Latin dance performances. Then a nice walk to a harbor followed. What a fun time.

## Pro Dinner

The US Go Congress is a popular place for professional players. Domestic professionals are invited to come and teach for some compensation, and Korean, Chinese, Japanese professionals come, supported by their national associations. Also, there are some professional players who come to the Congress for their own vacations. To show appreciation for all the professional players, the AGA hosts a Pro Dinner as a custom. This year, however, there was a volunteer to host the dinner. Mr. Kunho Choi, the owner of LA Korean baduk club, was the one. Mr. Choi's club has been a home for Korean players in LA for a few decades.

The Pro Dinner was a Korean barbecue at the beach. Mr. Choi found and booked a place with a huge charcoal grill and three long wooden tables that could accommodate more than 40 people. For the food, he delivered a truck load of meats, vegetables, kimchi, rice, chicken, and many more Korean side dishes from LA. The food was amazing, and I could tell that everyone had a delightful time there.

## Closing Ceremony - Banquet

Having a banquet with the closing ceremony is one of the traditions of the US Go Congress. Players would get out of the Congress shirts and dress up like non-baduk players. This year, the Congress directors prepared an outdoor banquet. The venue was very nice with a small fountain and a tall bell tower, and the weather was as perfect as it had been. With Andy as MC, everything went smoothly. In the end, I think we didn't have enough food for everyone, but we still had a wonderful evening.

## The End

Ever since I chose baduk for my career, each game of baduk was like a war to me. Dense fog was laid on a broad plain, and I would be all alone feeling alert and tense. Watching the baduk players at the Congress, I felt a bit jealous because they were really enjoying the game. I suppose I was there to teach something to them, but I think I may have learned more in the end.

# A Good Tournament

OCTOBER 31ST 2011 — I have been busy since the beginning of the semester – the end of August. Given this, I'd been waiting for the weekend after mid-term exams for a break. With exams right around the corner, however, I received a phone call from Mr. Seo of the Korea Amateur Baduk Association (KABA). He officially invited me to come to the Korean Prime Minister's Cup International Amateur Baduk Championship (KPMC) as a guest professional player. This tournament was scheduled the very weekend I'd been eagerly anticipating. Although as an initial reaction my mind I shouted "Nooooo!", I soon recovered from the shock and thought, *It's an international baduk event. I should go.*

Thinking about it, I believe I made the right decision. Though I didn't get the break I wanted, it was wonderful to meet players and organizers from 70 different countries, including some old friends and colleagues. Besides, my work at the tournament wasn't so demanding. I would walk around, talk to people, and play VIP games with the Executive Vice President of Posco and the president of Pohang Baduk Association (Pohang was the host city of the KPMC). These tasks were easy, and I could relax somewhat at the same time.

As you may assume, I have been to a myriad of tournaments, be they professional, amateur, domestic or international. Consequently, when I go to a tournament I have certain expectations and often see what I expect to see. This year's KPMC wasn't an exception, but my experience was different this time. I was paying attention to the things I overlooked or didn't care about before. What was the purpose of this tournament? What will make this tournament successful? How does each element of this tournament affect the participants' experience? Intentionally or unintentionally, I suppose I am becoming a business major.

After observing and talking to the players, organizers, part-time workers, sponsors, locals and my professional colleagues, I learned each party had different angles and expectations for the tournament. Then one question came to my mind: What makes a good tournament? In the current system, almost every tournament is identical. If we change anything from the status quo, what should that be?

At the superficial level, everything seemed well organized at the KPMC. The tournament venue was a newly built sports and cultural arts complex. It was clean, spacious and functional. The hotel we stayed at was the best in town, and the meals and snacks provided were decent. A number of honorary guests such as politicians, governors and the sponsors' VIPs paid visits to the grand opening ceremony. The organizers and part-timers, mostly from KABA or Myongji University, were efficient. Nevertheless, what people said in private or in person wasn't all bright. What were the problems?

## Players

In the KPMC, 70 players play six rounds over two consecutive days. This method is reasonable for most amateur tournaments, especially if you want to finish a tournament in one weekend. The KPMC, however, is an international tournament which makes many players travel for a dozen hours to attend. It may be a once-in-a-lifetime experience for many of them, and they definitely do not want to cram all the games into two days. The competition is very serious for a few top players, but for the rest of the players the experience is as important as their final scores. Therefore, we should look for a better balance between the *experience* and the *competition*.

## Organizers

Having a smooth, trouble-free event is important, but spending too much money preventing potential problems is equally troublesome. One staff member of the KABA told me that they considered having fewer games in a day, but the problem was limited resources and the difficulty of finding more sponsors. Cost controls were inevitable.

They shortened the tournament period, and restricted additional food and drinks at the dinner banquet. Instead, the hotel was luxurious, several professional players were invited, and there were polished stage performances at the opening ceremony. Although I was one of the guests myself, I had to question what the priorities were. What should be sacrificed and what should be kept?

## Sponsors

The media and the public are inured to reports of tournaments won by Korean or Chinese players. This makes it hard for a baduk tournament to get more than passing notice from the public. Therefore, it may be rational for sponsors to question the advertising benefit of sponsoring a tournament and their return on investment. In fact, this is why baduk tournaments are vulnerable. Most sponsors decide to be become sponsors because their leader likes baduk, or their predecessors made the tournament and they honor the tradition as long as it doesn't threaten the company's financial standing. I am not saying there is no return in sponsoring baduk tournaments. It's just not attractive enough to get non-baduk player sponsors. Thus, the question should be, *how will you get more publicity to attract prospective sponsors?*

## Professional Players

There were about six professional players in the tournament venue. They were all willing to help or talk to the participants, but the connection between the two parties was almost invisible. The language barrier was one problem, and the cultural expectations was another. In Korea, professional players don't offer a review or a teaching game unless you ask first. On the foreign players' side, professional players are intimidating, and they do not know how to ask for a review appropriately. What can bridge the gap? What will facilitate the interaction between them?

## Part-timers

Many of the part-time workers were there primarily to record games. Yet, recording games is so easy that almost all baduk players can do it effortlessly. On the other hand, the Myongji University students were strong baduk players themselves who were getting a professional education in Baduk Studies. It was a pity that such skilled workers were bored and unengaged most of the time. Isn't there a way to give them more challenging and meaningful tasks such as planning a side event for international visitors?

## Local contacts

The president of the Pohang Baduk Association proudly told me that they managed to hang banners advertising the KPMC all over the city for about a month before the tournament. Also the female members of the association all came in full Han-bok (Korean traditional clothes), and served many kinds of snacks and tea. Yet, despite the local people's hospitality and engagement, I couldn't see any interactions between the international players, the organizers, and the local people. How can the organizers facilitate the engagement of themselves, the players, and the local people more meaningfully? After all, relationship building is one of the motivations for having this tournament in the first place.

I don't have the answers. I don't know what budget the event had, what the difficulties were, or what kind of choices the organizers had to make. What I can tell is there is room for improvement, despite the fine job done by all the organizers. We can approach tournaments in new ways. I feel the organizers were susceptible to patterns and traditions. I hope they will work to make every year's tournament better than the year before.

# A Hard Lesson

December 31ST 2011 — My trip to the KPMC was not only fun but also fruitful. I met someone at the playing venue, and the meeting led me to a new project. Do you remember that I wrote about Lee Sedol 9p's commentary book? I found his book very exciting and wanted to translate it into English for the baduk players around the world.

Last year when the book came out, I sent a message to the author, Lee Sena. My passion and admiration for the book convinced Sena, and she asked for some sample translation work. I found a native speaker who liked baduk to help me edit, and together we did work that I was proud of. After viewing my sample translation pages, the author gave me permission to translate the book. Everything looked so bright and fresh. I wanted to make the Korean version of *Invincible*, the baduk book famous for its beautiful English and interesting content. In contrast to my excitement, however, the responses of publishing companies were stiff. I sent letters to several publishing companies, and while they were interested in having the book, they would not pay for the translation. The plan went dormant.

At the last KPMC, though, I met someone from a publishing company that shared my excitement for the book. They contacted me about a week later. A meeting was arranged, and the writer, people from the company, myself, and my editor convened. We discussed major terms of the contract, and set milestones for the progress of the work. Though it was still in the middle of my semester, it was the work I've been eager to get. I had no complaints, just passion and ambition. Everything was going exactly as I'd dreamed.

Then, things started to go wrong. After weeks of discussion about terms, contracts, translation issues, and more, the publishing company notified me today that they will cut me out of the project. I was hurt at first. Thinking about it now, however, I realize I learned many lessons, and I am now free to do something more exciting. I'd like to pass along some of the lessons, in case anyone reading this had ever considered doing translation work. I hope you can benefit from my experience.

First lesson was that the publishing companies can be very aggressive with their schedule. Just like I was excited and had ambitious goals for my translation work, the publishing company had their blueprint for a successful publication. They wanted to launch the book before the European Go Congress in Germany next July, so they had to have the book ready and sent to the printer well before that. The problem was that I considered myself a part-time translator and a full-time student, while the company's timeline demanded a greater commitment. What happened was this: I sent them my translation of the first section, and I had two weeks for the second section, but they sent me back my first chapter with a few hundred comments and questions. I answered all their questions for the first section, only to receive more questions. I told them I needed an extension of the deadline for the second section or postpone the revision process until I could finish translating the entire book by the due date they gave me. At this request, the publishing company decided to cut me off and have its in-house staff provide the translation. The funny thing was that I had a translator's contract, but it hadn't been signed yet. I was living in Daejeon, and we agreed it could be signed at a convenient time.

This problem could have been solved by having the translation work done before contacting the publisher. Then, they could perform their quality control and send the finished file to the designer and printer according to their own schedule. I could have translated on my own timetable and provided the attention to detail and quality that I thought the project deserved.

The lessons I learned around translation were no less significant. Understanding what was written was easy, but articulating it into English was not. I could explain the meaning to someone else if I was having a casual conversation. Writing is different. My primary concern was that a literal translation often failed to deliver the same weight as the original sentences do. The purpose was clear: to allow readers of the English version to get as much as Korean readers would get from the book. During the translation, I learned three issues which actively got in the way.

The first issue was clarifying. The commentary was for high level players, but we wanted players of intermediate levels to be able to learn from this book as well. My editor plays baduk, but is not too strong yet, so he was a good test to see if we were communicating with lower-level players. While he worked, he would ask me the meaning of sentences to make sure he preserved them when he refined my translation work. In the process, I realized many of my explanations or statements had unstated premises or rationales that may be obvious to strong players, but were not quite clear to the players under a certain level. One easy example would be this: "Black 2 to 14 is a joseki, but in this situation the result is good for Black." Seemingly simple statement as it is, there are some hidden elements here. If we expanded this:

- A result of a joseki should be even (assumed)
- Black 2 to 14 is a joseki.
- Black's potential territory in one area and white's advantage in the other should be equal. (unstated)
- The circumstances here made Black's position on the upper side better than what White gained on the right side. (unstated)
- The result in this situation was good for Black.

I admit that I sometimes took liberties using my professional status, and added explanations and clarifications where I thought they were needed. Some people might argue that would be beyond the translator's authority. They may be right. My value or purpose, however, dictates that the most important aspect is whether the readers got the message the author intended to convey. It is like a professor's lecture and her teaching assistant's review. When students get lost in the main lecture and come to the review, the TA may show them the hidden bridges between the professor's statements, because the TA understands both the professor's language, and the students' language.

Repetitive use of certain expressions was another hurdle. Baduk books, especially in the Korean language, are very generous with repeating the same words or expressions. For example, expressions such as "it is playable", "the result is good for Black", "it is well-balanced", and "Black A instead of 27" are so common that you are likely to encounter one or two of them in every paragraph. As you well know, however, English language in general has very little tolerance for repetition. Therefore my editor and I had to think about many synonyms or alternative expressions to replace some of these common phrases. We used "the exchange benefits Black", "the move produces a favorable outcome for White", "It is acceptable for both", and so on.

The third issue was with certain Korean-style perceptual terms, which have multiple meanings depending on the context. These words may have literal equivalents in English, but do not imply the same meaning as the Korean words offer. As I was facing those words, I scrutinized the roots of the words and the best way to express them. One solution would be to pick the closest word, and keep using it. Readers might grasp the meaning by the time they finish reading the book. Another one, which I preferred, was to use one or more specific words depending on the situation. For instance, "doo-tuh-un" may be translated literally as "thick," but it can also mean "safe," "slow," "strong," "having potential," "influential," and so forth according to the context in which it was used. Therefore, I could say, "Black 17 is thick" whenever I see the word in Korean, or "Black 17 solidifies his position while securing territory on the upper side" depending on the context. .

I don't just want to translate baduk books. I wanted to translate this particular book because I thought it was worthy of what I could bring to it as an English user and professional player. Though I have lost the chance to translate this book, I hope to someday find another book that excites the same passion and vision in me. If that day comes, I will hold these lessons closely.

# Backpacking in Japan

FEBRUARY 14<sup>TH</sup> 2012 — After the abrupt end of the translation project, I've been spending most of my time studying for the GMAT. The GMAT is a general aptitude test for graduate schools in business, and I was thinking about going to graduate school after SolBridge. Then about a two weeks ago, my little sister, Hayoung, came to me looking concerned.

Hayoung said, "Can you go to Japan with me?" She is majoring in Architecture for her undergraduate degree, and her professor recommended that they visit the Osaka area during winter vacation. Inspired by this, my sister has been preparing for the trip for months, writing down all the small details.

"What happened to your friend?" I replied by way of another question, referring to her schoolmate with whom Hayoung had been planning to travel.

"She can't go." I could tell that Hayoung was deeply disappointed, but I wasn't sure I could help because the test day for the GMAT was approaching. Also, I wasn't in the best financial state.

On the other hand, I wanted to support my sister. She obviously didn't want to travel alone, and it seemed almost impossible to find someone else soon enough. Another thing was that I have visited Japan several times already, but none of them were for fun. I went there only for tournaments, and would stay at the hotel for my matches. Then when the tournament was over I would come back to Korea with other players and the KBA staff members.

My sister, though, doesn't play baduk. She went to the baduk academy with me when she was 5-6 years old, but she didn't like to sit for a long time. Now she says she doesn't remember anything about it. My parents and I would sometimes encourage her to join a baduk club in her university, but she was not interested. Anyway, since she was not a player, the trip was guaranteed to be baduk-free, and I was intrigued by the idea.

Overall, the trip was much better than I hoped for. We visited castles and temples, as well as famous gardens designed by world-renowned Japanese architects. Japanese food was delicate and savory, though a bit pricey. The time together with my sister led to many conversations, allowed me to understand her better, and strengthened the bond between us. The legacy of family businesses was everywhere in the country, and provided a welcome counterpoint to Korea, where chains and franchises are driving out the old family businesses. Old ladies in shops and restaurants were almost overly kind.

I admit that this trip wasn't easy. Excessive walking and transferring on all kinds of public transportation exhausted me. The weather was windy and cold, making it harder to explore cheerfully. Many shops or restaurants refused to accept credit cards, and we found our cash reserves dwindling quickly. Most people we met in Japan spoke little English, and sometimes directions and information were written only in Japanese. Although we didn't have any "big" troubles thanks to Hayoung's thorough preparation, the backpacking was certainly tough, and I asked myself why I liked traveling.

Traveling often involves long flights, overburdened walking, struggling with a language barrier and cultural differences, as well as consuming a significant amount of time and money. In other words, you spend a thousand dollars and a precious one-week vacation to get to some unfamiliar places where you feel exhausted and frustrated. Nevertheless, people who have traveled before tend to travel again, while people who don't have this experience tend to wait for "the right time." Why would that be? I think the real benefits of traveling have an invisible nature. For example, traveling leads to sincere introspection by detaching yourself from daily life, appreciation of what you have, and better understanding of different cultures and countries.

Though my trip to Japan was a bit exhausting and costly, I would say taking the opportunity was the right decision. I am richer in spirit, experience, and perspectives. On top of that, I had quality time with my sister. Even when I get older, I hope I will choose to travel rather than being comfortable at home.

# International Coordinator

APRIL 5TH 2012 — Another semester has begun, and things are all going as usual. I do feel that my classes are getting more difficult, but I am managing them well so far. In the meantime, the weather has been warming lately. Since April came, I've been noticing the air is fresh, spring flowers are blossoming, and pleasant sunshine is everywhere. "The uncertain glory of an April day!" Shakespeare claims.

There's been a new change in my daily routine, by the way. As of February 1st, I started working part-time as an International Coordinator for the Korea Baduk Association (KBA). My main tasks are to promote the activities of the KBA around the world and to facilitate communication between the KBA and other Go associations. For example, I have been communicating with the European Go Federation and the Czech Go Association lately through emails on behalf of the KBA. It's been only two months, but I feel this work suits me better than playing in tournaments.

The whole change started with my first trip to Europe in 2006, to visit the Korean Ambassador's Cup tournaments in Germany, France, and the Netherlands. The trip was for three weeks, and our itinerary also included the UK, Austria, and Belgium. I had been a professional player for a year and a half then, and I spoke very little

English. I was fascinated by the charm of Europe and the passion European players had for Baduk. Though they weren't as strong, they were as sincere as any players in Korea. Many players were kind enough to try to communicate with me despite the language barrier. I regretted that I couldn't speak English better, and started studying it as soon as I came back to Korea.

The first step is the hardest, as the well-known adage goes. I have had many more chances since that first one. This was partly because I had experience, and partly because I learned English. After the Korean Consul General's Cup in Seattle in 2008, I went to the 2009 US Go Congress in Washington DC, the Kent School in Connecticut, the Korean Ambassador's Cup in Prague, the 2010 European Go Congress in Finland, the Polish Summer Go Camp, and the 2011 US Go Congress in California. Through these experiences, I became acquainted with many players and organizers around the world, and gained some understanding about the international Go scene.

As a junior student in an undergraduate program, I am still exploring options for my future career. No matter where I go or what I do, however, I want to be contributing to the baduk community in one way or another. I hope this International Coordinator title provides me with a base from which I can explore the right place for me in my home profession.

## Skills Acquisition

AUGUST 28<sup>TH</sup> 2012 — I guess I am an optimistic person. During the semester I am happy to go to school, and during vacation I am happy to be free from school. In my free time, my favorite activity is to read books. Classical literature, novels, history, business, economics, psychology, sociology, or any interesting topic is good for me. This summer, I didn't take any teaching trips to the West because there were many pros volunteering for the trips, and I wanted them to experience the Western Go world. Again, I would have been happy to visit any of the Go Congresses, but I was also happy to stay home and read a lot of books.

Yesterday, I finished an amazing book called *Thinking Fast and Slow* by Daniel Kahneman, a psychologist who won a Nobel prize in economics. This book was a collection of his essays about his research, and I found most of them so insightful. There were many things that I want to discuss, but one thing that caught my attention more than others was a part about skill acquisition: "The acquisition of skills requires a regular environment, an adequate opportunity to practice, and rapid and unequivocal feedback about the correctness of thoughts and actions."

One challenging aspect of baduk as a hobby is that it's difficult to improve your skills. Generally speaking, the higher level you are, the harder it is to become stronger. In my observations, though, everyone has a certain level at which they get stuck. At this point, it often takes years to rise to the next level. I have met many amateur players who have played for longer than a decade, but are not as strong as you expected them to be. They would tell me that they were 3-kyu for five years, or 1-dan for seven years. Though it is true that you don't need to be a strong player to enjoy this game, no one would deny that the real excitement comes from getting better and stronger.

Not surprisingly, questions such as "How did you study baduk?" or "What is the best way to improve my baduk?" tend to pop up more frequently in my conversations with amateur players. Among Korean players, the story of Master Cho Namchul's interview is quite well-known. In one interview, Master Cho was asked about a short-cut to improving baduk skill, and he said, "You tell me! If there is such a thing, I would like to use that myself." In my case, I used to answer in a vague way – "it depends on your level and playing style". It is a reasonable answer, but it can't be very satisfying. Yet, now I think I have a better answer to the question, "What should I do to improve in baduk?"

Prompted by *Thinking Fast and Slow*, I thought about an ideal program to help a player become stronger. In this program, one needs to take two lessons per week. In the first lesson, say on Monday, one learns something new – it can be in openings, reading, direction, or any other field. From Tuesday to Thursday, the player goes out and plays by herself, remembering what one learned from the lesson. The second lesson follows on Friday. This time it should be a game review so that the instructor can give feedback. It is essential that the instructor's feedback should be about both thoughts and actions, not just actions. In other words, the instructor should listen to the player's rationale and reasonings instead of just telling him/her better moves. Ultimately, what determines someone's level in baduk is how one thinks and reaches a conclusion for each move. Last, self-directed learning with books or video lectures on weekends will nicely back up the program.

Skill improvement doesn't come easily. Neither does a higher level in baduk. Yet, when you realize you are thinking differently, or when you see that higher rank on your name tag, you will know your efforts have been worthwhile.

## Twenty-Five Reasons Why You Should Play Baduk

OCTOBER 11<sup>TH</sup> 2012 — I've been enjoying my classes at SolBridge, but there is one area that I don't feel comfortable: Marketing. It's hard to motivate myself to make the extra effort on a marketing project unless I truly believe in what I am working for.

If I were a marketing manager for baduk, though, things would be different. I believe baduk is the best game in the world, and it deserves to be more recognized and enjoyed. It may not be everyone's game, but it can certainly be more accessible and approachable. Thinking about it, I decided to write down as many reasons as possible why people should play baduk. In the beginning I was hoping to find 100 reasons, but I couldn't get further than 25. Maybe I am not very talented at marketing after all.

## 25 reasons why you should play baduk

1. Its depth is fascinating. The board is limited and the rules are straightforward, but the number of possible variations is enormous.

2. Every game is a unique adventure. You can easily record your games, and revisit them any time.

3. You can play it indoors, outdoors, on the web, on paper, with tablets, smartphones, or even without any equipment using the coordinates.

4. It fosters active thinking. When you are playing, it's not an option to be passive as you could be if you were sitting in a classroom or watching a movie. You need to actively engage yourself in the thinking process, and it trains you to become an active thinker.

5. It's a sustainable game. Financial or physical hardships won't affect your ability to enjoy this game.

6. It resembles life. You have control over your choices, you predict what is going to happen, and you make plans. Then, it often doesn't work as you planned because you can only control yourself, not your opponent.

7. It is the oldest game in the world that is still played widely today. By playing this game, you can share your hobby not only with today's players, but all the players who've existed throughout some 4,000 years of history.

8. There is respect for opponents as a core part of the game. The winner understands the pain of the loser, and the loser tries to be happy for the winner.

9. You study openings, josekis, reading, counting, directions or tesuji all separately, but you must treat them as a whole when you play an actual game. It's the same in management in that you can study finance, accounting, HR, marketing, and IT separately, but you need to see them as a whole in order to lead an organization.

10. It teaches you that there can be more than one answer.

11. A number of research studies suggest that playing baduk prevents mental illnesses, such as dementia or memory impairment.

12. It inspires artists, writers, business people, politicians, mathematicians and philosophers.

13. Through playing in countdown, you get to practice decision-making under time pressure.

14. It forces you to think in your opponent's shoes, and this can improve your communication skills.

15. It becomes more interesting the longer you play or the stronger you become.

16. It's easy to have a favorite playing style such as territory-oriented or fighting-oriented, but depending on the opponent, you may be pushed to play in a different style.

17. Players' playing styles often reflect their personalities.

18. When you are nervous, angry, tired, excited, or annoyed, even if you pretend everything is fine, your moves can show your disturbed emotions.

19. It's easy to feel attached to games, or stones on the board, as if losing them would be the end of life. But, you learn that what you lose is just stones, nothing more. You can always start over.

20. It's a wonderful vacation game. You may play it in mountains, beaches, or a forest. All you need is a portable set, a partner to play with, and a relaxed mind.

21. It is a long-term game. One game easily involves a couple hundred moves, and you cannot sprint that long.

22. In order to be a strong player, you need both logical and emotional approaches to solve problems in actual games.

23. Your curiosity and experiments may not lead to good results at the moment, but they eventually reward you with improved skills.

24. It teaches that cramming before a test doesn't work. In order to win or get stronger, you need the discipline to practice regularly.

25. There is no such thing as beginner's luck. It may be possible for a beginner to win in other games because she is smart or athletic, but not in baduk. You really do need to work at it.

# Experience India

FEBRUARY 14TH 2013 — After finishing another semester successfully, I received an invitation from SolBridge to join its market research team on a trip to India. This was already the third overseas trip funded by my school. The first one was to Hong Kong, the second one to Taipei last year, and now to Delhi. These trips were offered as a reward for top students. In a way, I can say I earned these trips, but I feel I was lucky to be in the right place at the right time. I was born in the year of the dragon, on the day of the summer solstice. According to a Korean folktale, a dragon flies into the sky on the summer solstice. So my mom's friend told her that I would be traveling all around the world. Looking at myself travelling about as a tournament player, baduk teacher, and now as a college student, I wonder if my mom's friend really knew something.

After nine and a half hours of staring at a tiny monitor in front of me, I found myself in the heart of India, Delhi. A territory with rich history and culture, Delhi welcomed us with its newly built, shiny airport. Thrilled and excited by the impending adventure, my eyes devoured the rather typical scenes of duty free shops, lines of people waiting for immigration, and nondescript baggage conveyor belts. I knew India was only one of many foreign countries, but my intuition whispered there was something special about this place.

With dust blowing everywhere, I smelled a non-urban flavor in the air. At first it was strange to encounter a dog wandering by without a caregiver in sight. Then as I traveled around, I found more dogs, cows, pigs, horses – also by themselves, taking their place on the streets as if they had always been members of society equal to humans. At least the buses looked proper and the roads, decent. Soon, though, I realized one or both of the two were not adequate. The bus was constantly shaking and jumping. Chaotic traffic did not help. Small and large cars, buses, bikes, motorbikes, rickshaws, people, and animals all claimed their share of the poor road. There, the incessant cries of automobile horns were the only thing that maintained any order in the tangled traffic.

Do you consider yourself poor? In India, however many reasons you have to believe you are poor, you can still become appreciative of what you possess, unless all you have are some ragged clothes and the right to air and sunlight. Encountering countless beggars and homeless people, I couldn't feel more humbled and fortunate. After all, you don't need so much to live. The more you have, the greedier you are likely to become, sages say.

The complexity of Indian music and food was intriguing. Such a wide range of mixes that make up one entity, but deep inside, each element seemed complete unto itself. It was a system, not a collection. The Indian business market, likewise, was complex. A lot of languages, several religions, and different social classes coexist under the umbrella of India. On top of that, distribution and logistics is a big challenge. The managing director of LG India told us that a shipment from the east to the west coast of the US takes only three days on the road, but in India it takes 12 days. Hardly surprising if you had a chance to spend hours in a bus there, though. How would you deal with these challenges? I guess this is why India is the land of opportunity for entrepreneurs.

Indian people mostly seemed relaxed. They smiled easily and were hardly in a hurry even when they were late. In contrast, though, *fiercely competitive* was the expression that stuck in my mind during my time in India. It's probably the demographics of the Indian population that generates the competitive atmosphere. Out of 1.2 billion people in India, 70% of them are under 35 today. To acquire better education, better jobs, and better quality of life, they have to compete with each other in a pool of 840 million young people.

Observing many kids and young students wandering around streets without much to do, I thought about promoting baduk in India. This is the country where chess was born, and Indian students were known to be strong at mathematics. I understand that playing baduk wouldn't bring them food or anything productive, but if a baduk community were to develop, it could provide entertainment, educational value, jobs, and certain social benefits as well.

I can hardly say I know anything about India. What I do know, though, is that India asks you a lot of questions before you ask her any.

# My Valedictorian Speech

JUNE 18TH 2013 — I am graduating! Equally exciting, I am graduating a half year early, and as the Valedictorian of my graduating class no less! I guess it proves that the sacrifice of my tournament career wasn't for nothing. Thinking that I am leaving the school soon, I can't help looking back and feeling emotional. Riding my bike along the river for my commute, having tuna sandwiches and cappuccinos at the school café, rehearsing presentations with teammates in an empty classroom, or just hanging out with my friends and professors were all memorable in their own ways. I didn't consider them special when they were happening, but now each moment feels so precious.

When I was still a freshman, I attended a graduation ceremony, though I had no one specific to congratulate. There, one Chinese girl gave a valedictorian speech that left a strong impression on me. Later, I told one of my professors about it, and he said, "I have no doubt that you will be giving the speech when you graduate." Back then, it sounded like a dream. The professor didn't know of my background in baduk, or that I had spent most of my time studying baduk instead of math or science at school. In my school, there were students who graduated from elite high schools in their own countries or from high schools abroad like in the US. How was I going to outperform them outside the baduk board?

My time studying baduk hasn't been wasted. I learned that here at my school. The lessons and discipline that I gained from training could be applied to other fields too, and it made me strong. I don't believe it means I will have an easy time in a new field, but that I am capable of putting in the work required for success. Nothing will come without work and effort, of course.

Anyway, I would like to share the script for my speech at the graduation ceremony, since I put hours and hours to write and memorize it. I hope you will enjoy!

---

Chairman Kim, President Endicott, respected Professors, guests, and fellow graduates, thank you all for coming to share this liminal day of our lives. I am feeling ambivalent today; I am happy to move on to the next section of my life to put the skills and knowledge I have gained to use, but I am also sad to leave SolBridge. Dear SolBridge family, I will miss you greatly.

People say now is a tough time to graduate from college. The global economy is sluggish. Job openings are competitive. No, it is not the best time to be fresh graduates. I won't be so naive as to say everything will be fine. Yet, I can say one thing; we all developed the strength to compete in this world, and we will always have each other.

Today, we are celebrating our graduation from SolBridge. What does this degree mean to you? To me, a SolBridge degree represents great value.

I am confident that we learned patience from the elevator congestion. We have so many tools that we can now use for virtual collaboration in order to avoid the hassles of scheduling more team meetings. Sorry, that was a weak attempt to make a joke. We did have a lot of team meetings, and teamwork is something we have come to appreciate.

Jokes aside, I believe we truly had great experiences here at Sol-Bridge. Interacting with professors and classmates from all over the world opened our eyes as global citizens. We learned to communicate effectively in English. Many classes were demanding and rigorous which ensured we acquired knowledge and skills. Student clubs and activities provided opportunities for us to develop soft skills. The faculty and CEO mentoring program taught us invaluable wisdom that we couldn't have found anywhere else. For all of these, I would like to extend my sincere gratitude to Chairman Kim, Dr. Endicott, our professors and staff members for making them happen.

SolBridge was our choice, and we are happy and proud to receive a SolBridge degree.

Also, for my classmates and friends, I would like to share my small secret at SolBridge. I believe this is good time to tell you since I can be sure that it's too late for anyone to take away my valedictorian status.

One semester, I took 18 credits, had three part-time jobs, attended two non-credit classes, ran the student baduk club, and on top of that I tried to squeeze in time for my boyfriend and family. My calendar was always full. A few times, I sat with my then-mentor, Mr. Erick Mendoza, and discussed negotiables and non-negotiables to reduce my workload. Yet, I would say, "There is nothing to give up here!" I was busy, but I also felt happy and alive.

Can you guess what my secret was, other than that I had a supportive mentor? The secret was that I liked everything I did. I liked my classes, professors, classmates, classrooms, and everything else. Each morning, I was excited to start a new day. When there were too many assignments, I liked the thrill of the challenge. When there were few assignments, however, I liked the freedom. I loved my life.

You may be thinking, "Well, you were lucky to do what you liked." Before you jump to that conclusion, let me ask you this. If what you like and don't like is predetermined as if you rolled a die, what are the odds of liking all your classes while taking the 140 credits needed for graduation? Last Friday, I completed 143 credits, and I assure you that I liked each and every class I took as well as all professors that taught those classes. Was I just lucky to have only the classes I liked?

Here is the important part of the secret; I chose to like them. Jonathan Winters said "Nothing is impossible. Some things are just less likely than others." I would say, "Nothing is unlikable. Some things are just less likable than others." I believe the first ingredient for success is to like what you do. So, if you have a choice, choose what you like already. If you don't have the luxury to do what you know you like, remember that you can always choose to like it. Nothing is unlikable. Some things are just less likable than others.

I like all of you. Thank you for making it natural. I didn't have to choose.

# 2013 European Go Congress in Poland

AUGUST 12<sup>TH</sup> 2013 — My long journey at SolBridge ended with the graduation ceremony, but my journey as a baduk player continues! This summer, I was offered a trip to visit the European Go Congress in Poland, and I happily accepted.

### A Day at the Congress

The Congress site opens a new day with a round of the main tournament at 10 a.m. Players enter their playing room sooner or later and solemnly face the board. Each player gets two hours on average (top players get more time) plus 45 seconds three times of countdown for thinking time. This main tournament is the highlight of the EGC, and there are ten rounds over the course of two weeks. When I walked through the playing rooms, the atmosphere was so serious that I could almost hear each player's breathing.

While the Congress participants push themselves into the world of Go, the professional players enjoy some relaxing time in the morning. In my case, I would prepare for my lectures or hang out with some staff members in the registration office until noon, when the professional players' activities begin. There are simultaneous games, live commentary on the top players' games, or game-review sessions. I did each activity at least once, and noticed that live commentary was the most popular.

By around 2 or 3 p.m., most players had finished their games and would leave the main building for lunch. The most common place to go was the cafeteria. This place would serve one soup, one main dish, and a simple dessert like a small pack of fruit juice. The food wasn't fancy, but I liked that they served traditional Polish food. Another popular choice was the pizza place called Ravioli, next door to the cafeteria. Their pizzas were huge, while reasonably priced, and tasty.

At 4 p.m., there is a rapid tournament. There were nine rounds throughout the Congress, and players had 40 minutes and 30 seconds, with three times of countdown. Meantime, the players who weren't participating in this tournament would enjoy a long lunch break, go to the lake, play for fun, and hang out with other players at the main building. I would also talk to people, comment on their games or hang out at the office with the organizers.

Afternoon lectures by professional players started at 5 p.m. Ms. Guo Juan's lectures were as popular as always, so were Mr. Kim Sungrae's. They are both active teachers in Europe with decades of teaching experience. I once attended Ms. Guo's lecture, and I was amazed at how precisely she could name the expected mistakes of certain levels of players. My lectures, on the other hand, were more like lectures of a new lecturer in a university who had just finished her higher degree. I felt a bit nervous in front of large audience and made poor attempts at jokes which worked only half the time.

We had dinner from about 7 to 8 p.m., usually at the cafeteria. People didn't pay much attention to what they had for dinner, though, because in the evening we'd all go to the pub, also known as the "Evening Integration" place. This pub had nice beer on tap, and some cheese, potatoes and meat on a huge barbecue grill. We enjoyed beer and snacks, played Go or other games, had interesting conversations, listened to the guitar, or danced until we got too tired to stay any longer.

## Pair Go

You wouldn't believe how many side events can be organized in two weeks. At the EGC, every day looks similar but each day has something different. There were the Pandanet Go European Team Championship, the Pair Go Championship, Panel Discussions on the Future of Go in Europe, and a 9x9 tournament in the first week. The

Weekend Tournament followed – for short-term visitors – and the Phantom Go Tournament, Football Tournament, Volleyball Tournament, 13x13 Tournament, Rengo (six person) Tournament, and Children's Tournament were all held in the second week.

All side events are interesting in their own ways, but my all-time favorite is the Pair Go Championship. I believe Pair Go has special qualities and dimensions that individual play does not have. For one, it has the element of teamwork unlike conventional baduk. There is unspoken communication, tactics involving the playing order, constant revision of plans, and so on. This is why I have not missed Pair Go events in any of the Go Congresses I've attended so far.

This time I paired up with Cezary, a bright young Polish player. I met him for the first time in Warsaw three years ago, and we traveled together with his brother Mariusz to the Polish Summer Go Camp. We kept in touch after the camp through email, and over the past three years he became a college student while I finished my undergraduate degree. Also, he has made substantial improvement in Go, becoming 3-dan from 1-dan. Anyway, I wanted to play with someone I knew before, and fortunately he was available and willing to play with me.

We won three games in the preliminary round and four games in the main tournament, winning the first place of the Pair Go Championship. Afterwards, there were a couple of pairs that challenged us at the pub, but we still remained undefeated. It appears that we were a better team than I anticipated, and it was a lot of fun to play Pair Go with him.

## European Go Federation (EGF)

One of more memorable experiences I had this EGC was that I got to observe the Annual General Meeting (AGM) of the EGF. It was one thing to attend the EGC and interact with European Go players, but observing the AGM of the EGF was quite another in understanding the Go scene in Europe.

It is always a difficult question; do you change first to grow or do you wait until you've grown enough to change? Do you need professional players to develop the Go community in Europe or do you wait until the European Go community develops enough to have professional players? Will your top players become stronger with a professional league or will you wait until your top players become strong enough to compete internationally? Is this the right time to start? What is the worst that can happen if it turns out to be premature? What is the cost of waiting for a better time? I know that the American Go Association also went through these questions and has made a hard decision about setting up their professional system. About one year has passed, and we still don't know if it was the right decision. Yet, what I believed then and now is that the situation will never be perfect from the outset. As long as you have the organization and people that are willing to work through the hard environment, you should do it.

The creation of a professional system is an important matter for the EGF, but not the only matter. There were also heated discussions on ways to manage the EGC, governing policies, rating systems, etc. Observing as the meeting continued over six hours, I could see that the officers were not treating it lightly. They cared, and they had the best intentions to reach better conclusions. I was excited to see the AGM of the EGF for the first time, and I am still excited to see more of them in coming years.

## Question

"Is this Congress vacation or work for you?" A simple question, but I didn't have a simple answer. The player who asked it was looking at me with a curious smile. I took a moment to arrange my thoughts and said, "It feels more like vacation. I have to say, I have some work, but this is too much fun to be work." A few years ago, I would have said, "We are here for teaching. It's not a vacation." In fact, I was often frustrated when people thought I was on a vacation. I was there on behalf of the KBA, to teach and promote baduk. Not that I didn't have fun, but I kept the sense of responsibility inside me all along.

The responsibility has not faded away; it still resides in me. What changed was how I felt about it. It was just natural. During this Congress, I truly enjoyed discussing the future of Go in Europe, commenting on games, playing friendly teaching games, drinking beer with everyone, and so on. George Halas, an American football player and coach said, "Nothing is work unless you'd rather be doing something else." When I realized how much I was enjoying myself at the Congress, I couldn't call it work anymore.

# International Go Federation

SEPTEMBER 1ST 2013 — As I was going through my time in university, I changed my career plans several times. First I wanted to work for a management consulting firm, then I was interested in an investment bank or a large corporation like Samsung. When I was at my internship at the Embassy of Brazil in Seoul, I dreamed about moving to Brazil, too. As my last semester approached, though, I thought I wanted to continue my studies in finance. In Daejeon, there is a university called KAIST, one of the top schools in Korea. They have a finance program that combines a Master's and Ph.D. degrees. One professor of this program was a supervisor of the KAIST baduk club, where I have been lecturing for the last four years as a part time job. A few times I had a chance to interact with the professor, and he encouraged me to apply for the program. I could see myself enjoying a new life at KAIST, and my family and SolBridge professors all agreed KAIST graduate school was a good path for me. Then, something unexpected came up.

One day in my last semester, I received a phone call from the KBA. I was an International Coordinator, and we usually communicated on the phone. But this time, they asked me if I could come up to Seoul for a talk. I asked him what the talk was about, but he wouldn't tell me anything. So I took a train to Seoul one morning. To my surprise, it turned out to be a job interview. The current Secretary General of the International Go Federation (IGF) was resigning from her post, and KBA was asked to nominate her successor. For this post, they were looking for three qualifications: professional strength in Go, English ability, and international experience.

It was bizarre. I had said in my admission interview at SolBridge that I wanted to work for the IGF after graduating, but that I didn't know whether I would ever have the opportunity. I thought it could be a long-term goal that I may have a chance at after decades. But there I was, about to graduate, having an interview for a job at the IGF! It felt as if someone had been planning for it from the beginning. I knew the program at KAIST was a great career path in finance, but I couldn't possibly turn down this opportunity with the IGF. So, at the interview, I told them that I was ready to give up my other options if I got an offer from the IGF.

A few weeks later, I was called for a second interview with a higher manager in the KBA. He asked me about my school life and my experiences as a professional player, then gave me a one page document in Korean to translate into English. That was the end of the second interview. Before May, I was nominated as the next Secretary General of the IGF, and the KBA told me I could start getting the necessary training in September.

Only a few years ago, I was one of many young professional players. Yet, from the moment I decided to move back to my parents' place, I walked my own path. Walking this way has had its ups and downs as well as some challenges, but eventually it led me to the IGF today. It's still too early to say anything about this job, but I know that I will be happy to work with baduk organizers and use my talents to contribute to the development of the international baduk scene. For now, I am confident with my choice, and I can't wait to start my work!

# Appendix

*Selected Games*

# The 14<sup>th</sup> Women's Kuksu

Quarter-finals, played December 4, 2008

*White* | Lee Jihyun, 4*p*
*Black* | Lee Hajin, 3*p*

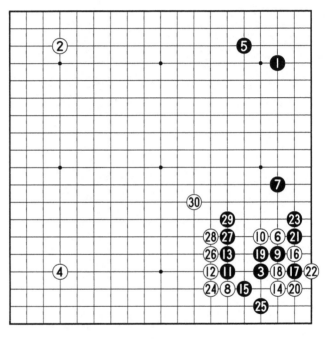

1 to 30.

Up to ㉚, white has built a wall on the lower side, but black has the right side and a potential Ko in the lower right corner. It's playable for both.

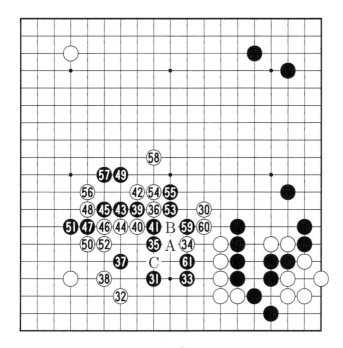

30 to 61.

④⓪ is an aggressive choice. ⑤④ would be a more common reply to
③⑨.

⑥① is necessary because of the threat to cut with white A, black
B, white C.

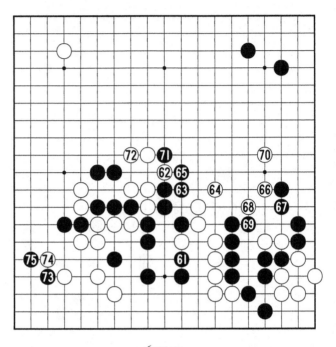

61 to 75.

⑦ is a good answer.

Black ⑦ and ⑦ are probing moves, before black sacrifices the two stones on the left side.

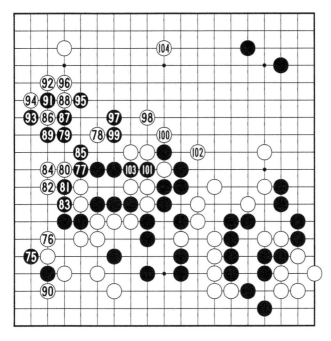

75 to 104.

⑧ and ⑫ are tesujis that force black to connect with a bad shape. After ⑩, white is ahead in territory.

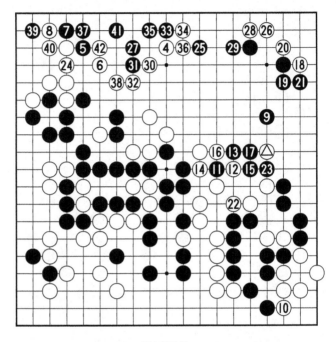

104 to 142.

Black **11** and **13** are tesuji. White's triangled stone was big.
The game became close after **41**.

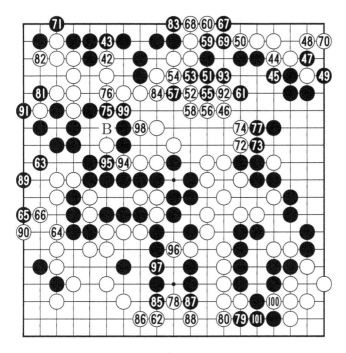

142 to 201.

White should have exchanged A and B before playing ⑦2.

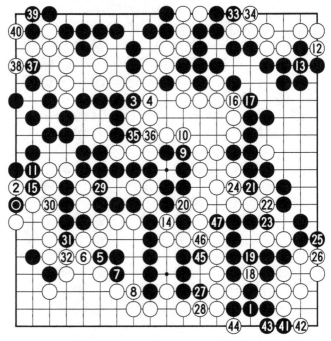

201 to 248.

248 at ◉

*Black wins by 0.5*

# The 14<sup>th</sup> Women's Kuksu

Semi-finals, played January 22, 2009

|        |                |
|--------|----------------|
| *White* | Lee Hajin, 3*p* |
| *Black* | Lee Minjin, 7*p* |

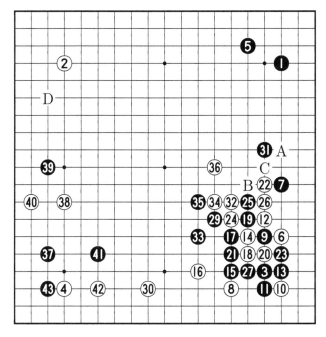

1 to 43.

㉘ at ❾.

㉚ could be played on A as well.

Instead of ㉝, if black saves the two stones at B, then white C would be a good move. This variation is good for white.

㊸ is slow. D would be better.

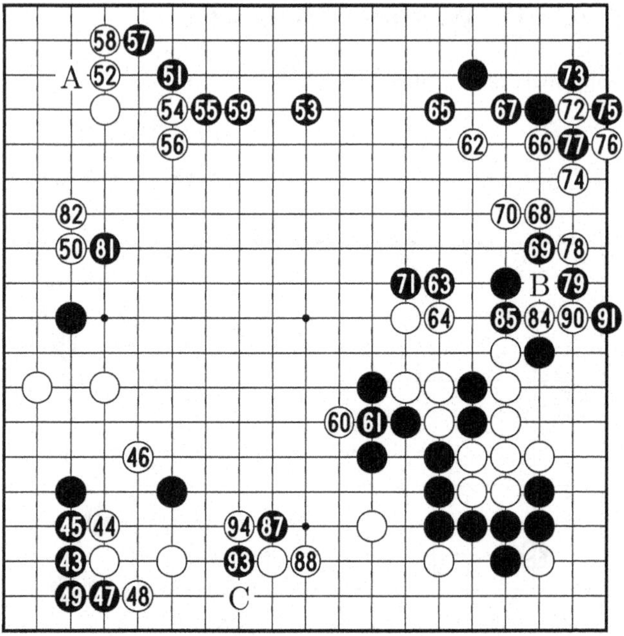


43 to 94.
80, 83, 86, 89, 92 at ko.

A is also a good option instead of 51.
85 would be better at B.
Instead of 94, white should answer at C.

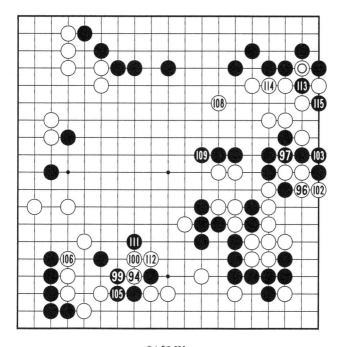

94 to 115.

(95),(98),(101),(104),(107),(110),(113) at ko.

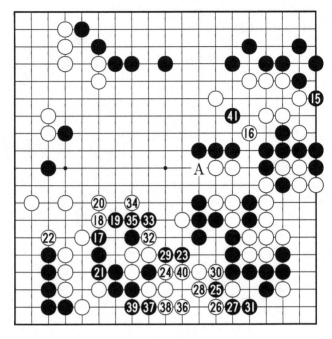

115 to 141.

White ⑫ should be played at ㉛.
Black is ahead up to ⑭.
Black ㊶ would be better at A.

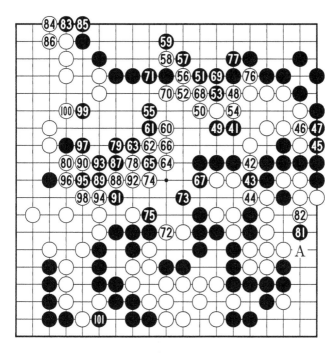

141 to 201.

The game became close at ⑱⓪.
㉑⓪ was smaller than 'A'.

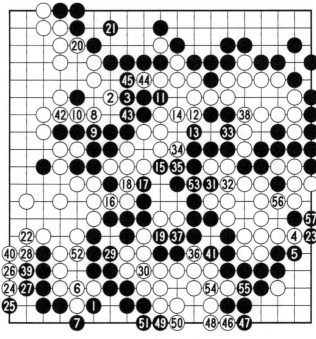

201 to 257.

215 should have been at 222.

*White wins by 0.5*

# The 14$^\text{th}$ Women's Kuksu

Finals, best-of-three, game 1, played February 20, 2009

|        |                  |
| ------ | ---------------- |
| *White* | Lee Hajin, 3*p*  |
| *Black* | Rui Naiwei, 9*p* |

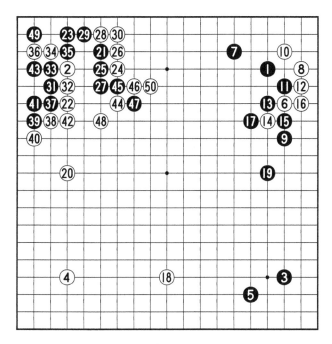

1 to 50.

㉘ should have been played at ㉞ instead.
The result in the upper left is good for black.

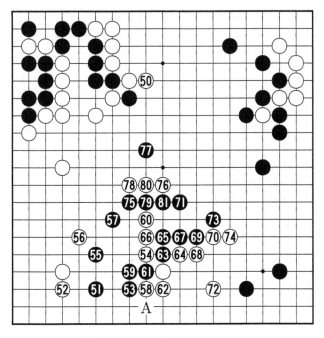

50 to 81.

White ⑤⑧ was better at A instead.

❻❸ is a severe cut.

❼❼ is a good move that drives the white stones into black's influence.

Black is clearly ahead after capturing the three stones with ❽❶.

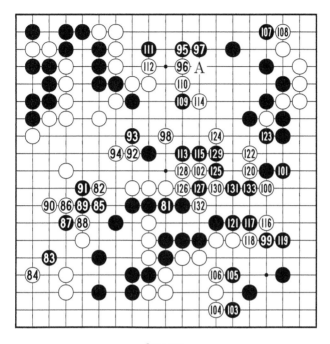

81 to 133.

Black **97** is a safe move. Usually hane at A is better.
**113** is sharp. White can't capture the black stone.

*Black wins by resignation.*

# The 14<sup>th</sup> Women's Kuksu

Finals, best-of-three, game 2, played March 9, 2009

*White* | Rui Naiwei, 9p
*Black* | Lee Hajin, 3p

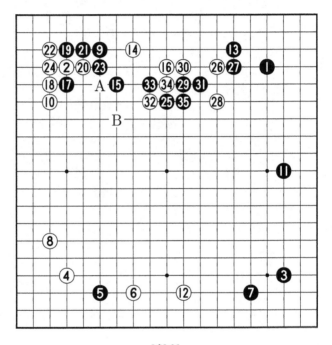

1 to 35.

**15** is an experiment. A more common response is at 'A'.
**29** and **31** are overplay. Black should have played at 'B' first.

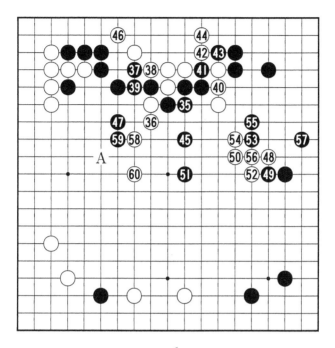

35 to 60.

㊉ would be better at 'A'.

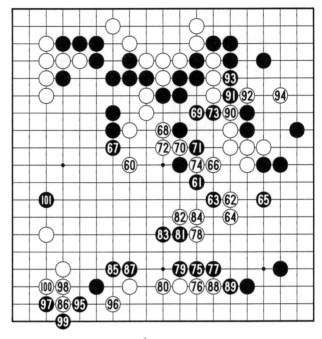

60 to 101.

Exchanging ⑥③ for ⑥④ was unnecessary.
White's cut at ⑦④ is thick and white is ahead.
Instead of ⑧⑤, black should have taken the corner at ⑨⑧.

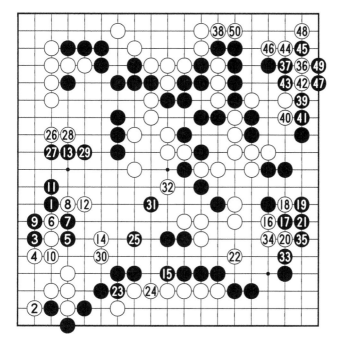

101 to 150.

White ⑭ is a safe move, and it's difficult for black to catch up at this point.

White ⑱ and ⑳ are a good tesuji combination for reducing black's territory.

With ㊿, the game is practically over.

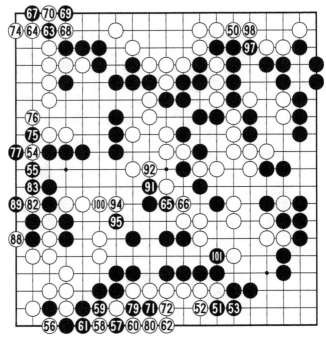

150 to 201.

⒙⒐ at ⒘⒐.

⒘⒊,⒘⒏,⒙⒈,⒙⒋,⒙⒌,⒘⒎,⒚⒑,⒚⒊,⒚⒍,⒚⒐ at ko.

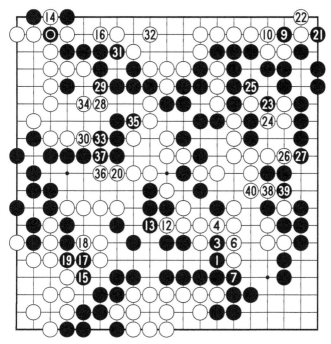

201 to 240.
202, 205, 208, 211, 214 at ko.

*White wins by resignation.*

# The 3$^{rd}$ GG Auction Cup

Main round, played April 29, 2009

*White* | Jimmy Cha, 5p
*Black* | Lee Hajin, 3p

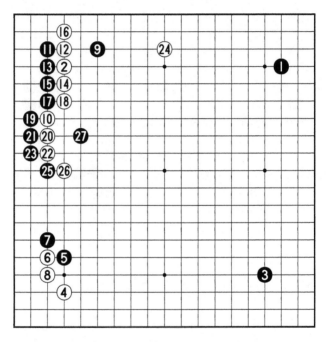

1 to 27.

Up to ㉔ is expected when ⑩ is played.
㉖ is more common at ㉗.

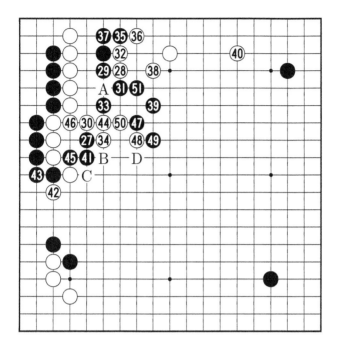

27 to 51.

㉙ is a sacrifice strategy. White can capture with the hane at A, but black will gain influence in the center.

㊽ was an overplay. It would be better to exchange B for C, then jump to D.

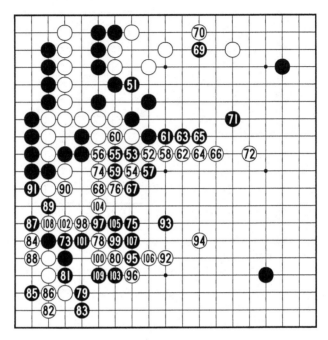

51 to 109.
Ⓐ at ㊹.

92 was too thin. Just playing at ⑩⑥ would be better. The three stones were important, and black is ahead with ⑩⑨.

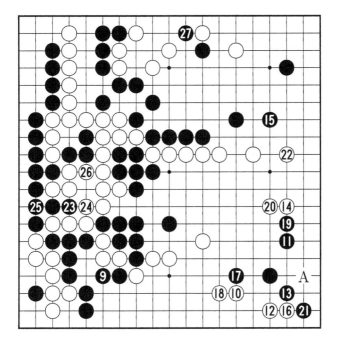

109 to 127.

Black exchanges ⑲ for ⑫⑩ to prevent A.

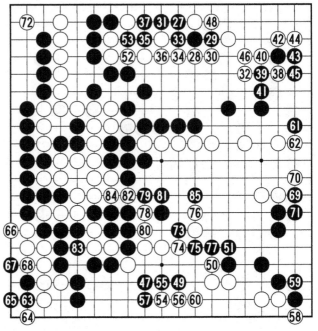

127 to 185.

With **147**, black is ahead in territory and white has little chance to catch up.

*Black wins by resignation.*

# The 12th Jeongkwanjang Cup

Qualification, final round, played November 5, 2010

| | |
|---|---|
| *White* | Lee Hajin, 3*p* |
| *Black* | Lee Jihyun, 4*p* |

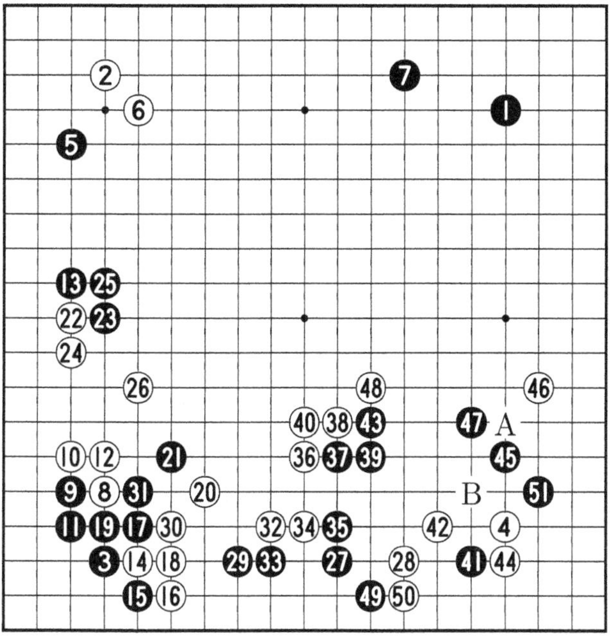

1 to 51.

⑯ is a territory oriented choice.

㊺ would be better at A.

(51) is a mistake. Black should have peeped at B.

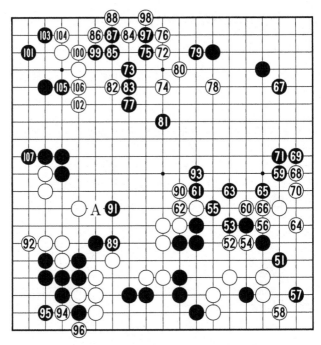

51 to 107.

**89** is slow. Black should attach at A and connect at **94**.

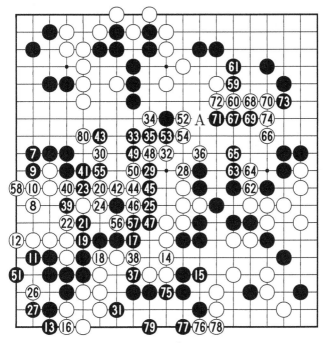

107 to 180.

⑳ would be better at ⓭.

⓭ is premature. Black should play at A first.

Up to ㊏, white managed both groups, and the game is practically over.

*White wins by resignation.*

# The 12th Jeongkwanjang Cup

Main round, played March 26, 2011

| | |
|---|---|
| *White* | Lee Hajin, 3*p* |
| *Black* | Rui Naiwei, 9*p* |

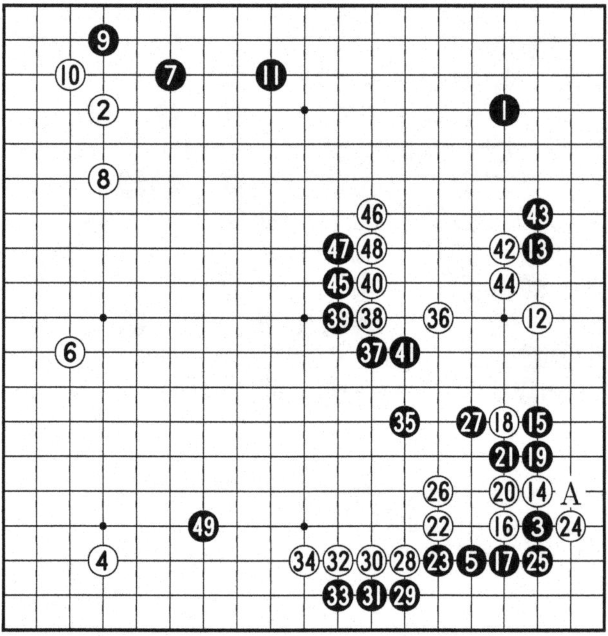


1 to 49.

⑥ is an unusual choice.
⓳ is more common at W24.
⑳ should be at A instead.
㊵ should have played at ❹1 first.
(51) is severe attack and black is ahead.

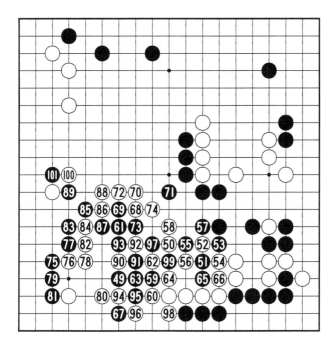

49 to 101.

**73** is painful for white, but **75** would be better at ⑦6.
⑧6 should have been at **93** instead.

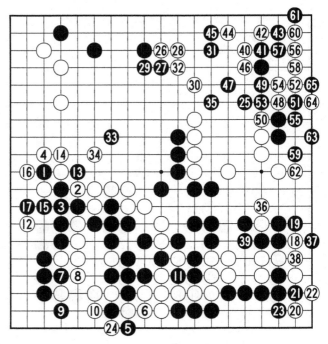

101 to 165.

Up to ⑫④ the result is good for black because black has sente.

⑭⓪ is an overplay, but once black secures the corner white has no chance of catching up.

❹❺ is the best answer, and the game is over.

*Black wins by resignation.*

CPSIA information can be obtained
at www.ICGtesting.com
Printed in the USA
LVOW04*0419230316
480378LV00008B/46/P